Revelation

The People's Bible Commentary

REVELATION

Marcus Maxwell

The Bible Reading Fellowship
OPENING THE BIBLE

Text copyright © Marcus Maxwell 1997

The author asserts the moral right to be
identified as the author of this work.

Published by
The Bible Reading Fellowship
Peter's Way, Sandy Lane West
Oxford OX4 5HG
ISBN 0 7459 3297 5
Albatross Books Pty Ltd
PO Box 320, Sutherland
NSW 2232, Australia
ISBN 0 7324 1656 6

First edition 1997
10 9 8 7 6 5 4 3 2 1 0

Acknowledgments
Unless otherwise stated, scripture quotations
are taken from the New Revised Standard
Version of the Bible copyright © 1989 by the
Division of Christian Education of the
National Council of the Churches of Christ in
the USA.

A catalogue record for this book is
available from the British Library.

Printed and bound in Great Britain
by Cox and Wyman Limited, Reading

Contents

Introduction (1)		6
Introduction (2)		7
1	Blessed readers	16
2	Postmarked heaven	18
3	Overwhelming vision	20
4	The holder of eternal life	22
5	Ephesus—love and doctrine	24
6	Smyrna—poverty and riches	26
7	Pergamum—the devil's capital	28
8	Good neighbours or witnesses?	30
9	A new name	32
10	The growing church	34
11	Trusting in God	36
12	Judgment and victory	38
13	Church of the living dead	40
14	Faithful church	42
15	Pillars of the faith	44
16	Successful Christians?	46
17	Love and glory	48
18	God himself	50
19	Heaven and earth	52
20	Spirit of creation	54
21	The song of creation	56
22	The great reversal	58
23	The Lamb enthroned	60
24	Crescendo	62
25	The seven seals	64
26	Violence	66
27	Famine and death	68
28	Call for justice	70
29	Standing before God	72
30	Belonging to God	74
31	Ready for battle	76
32	The company of heaven	78
33	Strange conquest	80
34	Return of the exiles	82
35	Prayer and fire	84
36	The earth recoils	86
37	Swarm of torment	88
38	The wages of sin	90
39	The failure of judgment	92
40	Turning point	94
41	Word from heaven	96
42	Bitter-sweet news	98
43	The dimensions of the Church	100
44	Faithful witnesses	102
45	The salvation of the world	104
46	Resurrection hope	106
47	God takes charge	108
48	The end of the future	110
49	Cosmic conflict	112
50	Mother of salvation	114
51	Gospel story	116
52	The devil's demotion	118
53	Wings of eagles	120
54	The Antichrist	122
55	Undermining evil	124
56	False prophet	126
57	The mark of the beast	128
58	Naming the beasts	130
59	Holy war	132
60	Eternal gospel	134
61	The coming Lord	136
62	Grain of joy, grapes of wrath	138
63	Exodus song	140
64	Final plagues	142
65	Nature in torment	144
66	Glamorous darkness	146
67	The weight of judgment	148
68	Beautiful evil	150
69	Mysterious beast	152
70	The beast decoded	154
71	The state of the beast	156
72	Luxury and desolation	158
73	In the world, not of the world	160
74	Self-pitying mourners	162
75	Cargoes of oppression	164
76	Idolatry and justice	166
77	Sad justice	168
78	Witness	170
79	Hallelujah!	172
80	Pre-emptive worship	174
81	The coming of Christ	176
82	The last battle	178
83	Millennium	180
84	Binding Satan	182
85	Church triumphant	184
86	Eternal consequences	186
87	Book of life	188
88	New creation	190
89	City of God	192
90	Eternal love, eternal life	194
91	Goal of creation	196
92	Beginning and end	198
93	Children of God	200
94	Beloved bride	202
95	Meeting place	204
96	Shining city	206
97	The never-ending story	208
98	Saviour of the nations	210
99	Water of life	212
100	True prophet?	214
101	Coming soon?	216
102	Yours faithfully	218
103	Come, desire of nations	220

Introduction (1)

For those who don't read introductions

If you are one of those people who tend to skip the introduction, welcome. There are just a couple things I'd like to tell you about this book before you begin.

Firstly, it is not a verse by verse commentary, and it doesn't have the text of Revelation in it. While it will make sense if it is read on its own, it assumes that you have the appropriate passage open, or at least fresh in your memory, while you read. The version it is based on (except in a very few places) is the New Revised Standard Version (NRSV), though any version will do.

Secondly, it takes the view, along with most scholars, that the book of Revelation would have been perfectly well understood by its first-century readers, and is therefore not a detailed blueprint of the plan of God for the Second Coming. It primarily addresses the churches of the Roman province of Asia Minor, and has to be understood as a message to them. At the same time, it is highly relevant to modern Christians, and carries a timely message to the world at the eve of the twenty-first century.

I hope you will find it helpful.

Marcus Maxwell
Advent 1996

Introduction (2)

It's very tempting, when we pick up a commentary, to skip the introduction. We want to get to grips with what the Bible says, or to prepare a Bible study or sermon, and the introduction is full of boring stuff about dates, authorship, geography, literary style, and so on. However, sometimes these are quite important, and help us to understand what the writer was trying to say, and how it may apply to us. This is especially the case with Revelation, which has been interpreted in lots of different ways, some of them so weird that many people have the impression that it is either irrelevant to modern Christians or the preserve of specialists.

In this introduction I want to set out very briefly the approach taken in this short commentary and explain why I think it is the best one. There will also be a few comments on dates, who wrote Revelation, why, and how the book is put together. If it is your first encounter in any depth with the strangest book in the New Testament, you will probably find it helpful. If you want more detail on technical matters of dating, authorship, and so on, you will find them in the introductions to the commentaries mentioned in the reading list at the end of this section.

What sort of book is Revelation?

At one time, many people thought that Revelation, together with the second half of Daniel, and to some extent, the visions of prophets such as Ezekiel and Zechariah, were a unique type of writing found only in the Bible. It was easy then to see them as a coded message about the future. This way of interpreting the book is still popular in some circles, which see it as a detailed prediction either of the history of the world as a whole, or of the Church in particular. It is then usually seen as dealing mainly with the period immediately before the return of Christ. The symbolic language it uses is interpreted in the light of current events. For instance, the beast from the sea which we meet in chapter 13 is seen as the Pope, or Martin Luther, or Hitler, or Stalin or Ming the Merciless, or whoever the interpreter's enemy might be.

The good point about this way of looking at the book is that it does stress that Revelation is applicable to the Church of the present. It also reminds us that Christians look to the future, and the coming of God's kingdom. The big problem with it is that it assumes that John, the writer, was writing about specific events and people in the future far from his own time. This would mean that most of the book was irrelevant to the churches to which it is specifically addressed (chapters 2–3). It also means that it is in fact impossible to know who and what these future people and events are. Although writers throughout history have seen Revelation as portraying the events of their own time (the Thirty Years War, the First World War, the formation of the European Union) history has carried on without Jesus' return. It seems strange that the Bible should contain a book which is so impenetrable.

Another way of looking at the book is to see it as a collection of powerful, poetic images which stimulate Christian imagination and devotion. This is true as well, but there must be more to it than that. Otherwise, our imagination can run riot, and we can read into it anything we like. It seems strange that someone should write a book, which he claims is a message from Jesus himself (1:1–2) which can mean anything the reader wants it to mean.

In the last hundred years or so, scholars have realized that Revelation belongs to a particular style of writing which was popular in Jewish and Christian circles for about a hundred years before and after the time of Jesus. These books are known as 'apocalypses' from the Greek word, *apokalypsis*, which simply means 'revelation'. They take various forms, but between them they have certain recognizable characteristics. They are often written in the name of a famous teacher or prophet of the past, as though he had predicted the events of the real writer's time. The book of Daniel falls into this category. It was most probably written to encourage Jews of the second century BC but in the name of a famous figure of the exile to Babylon in the sixth century BC. This may seem dishonest to us, but was a recognized literary convention in the ancient world.

Apocalypses often claim to show the history of the world from the viewpoint of heaven. They tend to be given to the writer in the form of a message or vision brought by an angel, and they promise the mighty intervention of God, who will act to bring about his rule, and to save his people in a miraculous manner. Sometimes they are highly symbolic, though few are as laden with strange images as

Revelation is. Many such apocalypses still exist, and provide an important insight into Jewish and Christian thought in the period of the early Roman empire.

In recent years some scholars have begun to argue that the images of cataclysmic change in apocalyptic language are not really about 'the end of the world'. Instead, they should be seen as predicting, or even calling for, great changes in the social order. On this view, apocalyptic writing is as much a call for action by its readers as a prediction of God's intervention. It seems to me that to a great extent, both views can be held together. Certainly we shall see that as far as Revelation is concerned, it does deal with the end times, and the return of Christ, followed by the last judgment. It also makes a powerful call to the Church to live in the light of the coming Christ, and implies a call to model the present world on the coming kingdom.

It is clear, then, that Revelation belongs to the apocalyptic style of writing, and would be understood as such by its first readers. So it was definitely written to the churches in the Roman province of Asia Minor. At the same time, the writer makes it clear that he is writing a book for all the Church, and one which will have a lasting relevance to Christians. Of all the books of the New Testament, Revelation comes closest to being written as scripture. Its detailed interconnections with the Hebrew scriptures, the construction which consciously aims to repay detailed study and its repeated claim to be the very message of God himself suggest that John comes close to putting his work on the same level as the Old Testament. To say that it is a first-century apocalypse does not rob it of its significance. It gives us the key to understanding it. In this commentary we will treat it as a message to the churches of John's own time, dealing with the difficulties and temptations facing Christians in the Roman empire. We will also discover that it has a great deal to say to Christians in the world at the end of the twentieth century.

Date and author

It is hard to decide exactly when the book was written, but the best guess is probably near the end of the first century, about AD95, during the reign of the emperor Domitian. Because of Revelation's stress on persecution, it used to be said that Domitian was one of the great persecutors of the Church, but there is no independent historical evidence to suggest this. When John wrote, many would remember Nero's persecution of the Christians of Rome in AD64. John warns that worse is to come.

We know nothing about John, except what we can guess from Revelation. He is probably not the same John who wrote the Fourth Gospel, though he came from the same area and the same group of churches.

The symbolism of Revelation

John is steeped in the Hebrew scriptures, which he certainly knew in Hebrew, since his references to it seem to be his own translation, rather than the published Greek version of the day, known as the Septuagint. In his book, he seeks to tie together his vision of the role of the Church, and Jesus' message to it with the messages of the prophets of the Old Testament. He draws heavily on Daniel, Ezekiel, Zechariah, Isaiah and the themes of Exodus. Most of the symbols he uses are his reinterpretation of the symbols of the Old Testament. He could expect his readers to be familiar with their Bibles (our Old Testament) as well as with the stories and sayings of Jesus. Unlike most writers of apocalypses, he rarely explains the meaning of his symbols, leaving it to his readers' knowledge of the Bible. For this reason, we will make frequent references to the Old Testament, though not as many as a detailed study would require.

John's failure to explain the symbols in detail is quite deliberate. It allows them to carry several meanings, each of which can speak to the Church in different situations and at different times, though the overall message of the book is clear.

Revelation is very carefully written, though in a rather rough and ready Greek, which seems intended to give the book a 'biblical' feel. Detailed study shows that John was adept at the styles of biblical interpretation which were popular in his day, especially amongst Jewish writers. For those with a good grasp of the Hebrew scriptures, there are hidden layers of meaning within his writing. There is, however, no secret message for those with deep knowledge. John's clever biblical cross-references make exactly the same point as the book as a whole: that the Church is called to witness faithfully to Jesus and to resist the temptation to compromise with the world.

The structure of Revelation

John not only uses his biblical references carefully, he also puts a lot of effort into the way the book is constructed. To anyone who has read several commentaries on Revelation, this may seem a strange statement, since almost every commentator has his or her view of exactly what the structure is. This is because we tend to think of books as having a straightforward progression from the beginning, through the middle to the end. Revelation is not quite so simple. There is an introduction, a middle section and a conclusion, but within that there are repetitions, visions within visions and themes which seem to disappear only to re-emerge later.

John recounts the same events several times, expanding the detail, and providing fresh viewpoints. For instance, there are three series of seven judgments: the seals (beginning in chapter 6), the trumpets (from chapter 8) and the bowls (chapter 16). At first sight these are successive events, but on closer examination turn out to be different perspectives on the same thing, since all end at the last judgment. The overall effect is not so much a road which passes through various points en route, as a net of interconnected symbols and events with layers of meaning.

A second feature of the book's structure is due to a fact which modern readers easily forget: it was written first and foremost to be listened to, not simply read. Those who did read it in detail would be repaid by the depth of meaning we mentioned above. Most hearers, though, would need signals to help keep them on track. For this reason, John uses numbers (and multiples of them) with special significance: seven means completeness, four refers to creation, two is the number of witness, twelve is the people of God. These numbers would be well known, and are drawn from the Bible and Jewish tradition. John uses repeated phrases (always with a slight variation) to tie together related passages. For instance, the peoples of the earth are described in variants of 'every tribe and tongue and people and nation' which would act as a reminder to those who heard the book read out.

Sometimes he links passages together by beginning the second section before he has ended the first one, rather like the hooks on a model train. A good example of this is 8:2 where the angels with seven trumpets are introduced, and then the preceding vision of seven seals is finished off in 8:3–5.

Another trick is to insert one series of visions inside another. The vision of heaven in chapters 4–5 is followed by the seven seals of 6:1—8:3, but it is broken by chapter 7 which returns us to the world of the saints and a vision of worship before we come back to the judgments on earth. In this way, John holds together his message about the judgment of the world and his vision of the role of the Church.

One section which is not tied to any other is chapter 12, where he makes a new start. In fact, the theme of the chapter picks up from chapter 11. In order to explain chapter 11 more fully, he goes further back in time, and so signals that with an abrupt change.

The book as a whole is written as a single letter to the seven churches. Like all letters of the period, it has a certain type of greeting and conclusion which frame the book as a whole.

The book as a whole has one very important structural feature. Chapters 10–11 form the centre-piece of the work, around which the rest is constructed. The first nine chapters lead up to it, and the last ten chapters explain it and draw out its consequences. It is in these two chapters that the (literally) central message of the book is found.

A brief outline of Revelation

The complex structure of the book makes it possible to pick out various patterns which may be mistaken for the one and only pattern of the whole composition. It is better simply to sketch an outline of the major sections and then pick up themes as they appear.

1:1–8	Introduction
1:9–20	Introductory vision of the risen Lord
2:1—3:22	Jesus's messages to the seven churches
4:1—5:14	Introductory vision of heaven leading to:
6:1—8:1; 8:3–5	Seven seals
(7:1–17	The role of God's people)
8:2; 8:6—11:19	Seven trumpets
(10:1—11:14	The role of God's people—and the central message of the book)
12:1—14:20; 15:2–4	The battle between the people of God and the forces of evil
15:1; 15:5—16:21	Seven bowls
17:1—19:10	God's victory over Babylon

19:11—20:15	Judgment of the world and the victory of the saints
21:1—22:5	The new creation and the city of God
22:6–21	Conclusion and final greetings

Further reading

A lot has been written on the book of Revelation, much of it useful, but a fair bit of it very misleading. Readers who are familiar with the literature will be able to tell what I have read (and, more embarrassingly, what I have not!) This commentary is intended as an introduction to the book, and if you want to read more, the following few titles will be useful.

The books which have most helped me to form my own views are both by Richard Bauckham:

The Theology of the Book of Revelation, New Testament Theology Series, Cambridge University Press, 1993 is a short but comprehensive guide to the thought and message of the book.

The Climax of Prophecy, Studies on the Book of Revelation, T. & T. Clark, 1993 is an academic work dealing in depth with some of the issues of the first book. Very heavy stuff, for the reader who knows Greek. Some Hebrew is helpful too.

John Sweet, *Revelation*, SCM Press, 1979 is a very good commentary and is readable with it.

G.B. Caird, *The Revelation of St John the Divine*, Black's New Testament Commentary Series, A. & C. Black, Second Edition, 1984 is a beautifully written commentary full of theological and devotional sensitivity.

Robert W. Wall, *Revelation*, New International Biblical Commentary, Hendrickson Publishers, 1991 attempts to relate the message of Revelation to scripture as a whole.

More popular commentaries include the following:

Michael Wilcock, *I Saw Heaven Opened*, The Bible Speaks Today Series, Inter-Varsity Press, 1975 is a straightforward attempt to explain the relevance of the book to modern Christians.

Murray Robertson, *The Future of Humanity*, Albatross Books/Bible Reading Fellowship, 1993 is a pocket-sized commentary which applies John's message of spiritual warfare to the structures and concerns of today. Unfortunately, it does not deal with the first three chapters, as these were assigned to a companion volume.

From these few works, anyone who gets addicted to studying Revelation will be able to locate hundreds of other titles.

A brief personal note

I have gained great pleasure, a good deal of benefit, and some frustration in the writing of the present book. For all this, I would like to thank the series editors for asking me to write it, and the authors of all the books and articles I have read, who cannot be listed here. There are bound to be mistakes and misunderstandings in what I have written. Where these have not been borrowed from other writers, they are entirely my own!

Thanks too, to Brian Lipscombe and Jason Boyd for commenting on parts of my manuscript. Sometimes I even took their advice.

Finally, thanks to my family, Sarah, James, Laurence and Polly for their encouragement and patience. The finished product is dedicated to them.

Marcus Maxwell
Advent 1996

1 Blessed readers

John begins his book by explaining what sort of work his readers are to expect. It is a 'revelation' (verse 1) or apocalypse which has come, not simply from John himself, but from Jesus Christ, the risen Lord of the Church, who in turn is conveying God's message.

To the first readers or hearers of the book, this would explain what type of literature to expect. Firstly, it would be an apocalypse, dealing with the events of earth and heaven and the last days, and secondly, it was a prophecy (verse 3)—a message from the risen Lord to his Church.

While apocalypses took many forms, John's original audience would not be surprised, and might well expect, to find the message conveyed in rich and wonderful symbols, which they would recognize from their knowledge of scripture and their experience of similar kinds of writing. However, they would most certainly expect to find a message of relevance to them, for this was a prophecy.

To us, prophecy tends to mean a foretelling of the future, and there is some of that in Revelation. But that is too narrow a view of prophecy. The biblical prophets, and the prophets of the early Church, intended their message to speak to the situation of those who first heard it. So Revelation claims to be a message from Jesus to the Christians of the seven churches in Asia Minor to whom it is addressed.

Witnesses

These opening verses also signal the main theme of the book—witness. John is a witness who bears testimony to what he has seen and heard, and he received it via an angel (whom we do not meet until chapter 10) from Christ, who in turn bears witness to the truth of God. Indeed, in verse 5 Christ is described as the 'faithful witness'.

The great calling of the Church is to be a witness, to proclaim in word and deed the message of the gospel; to tell out to the world what God has done. In being witnesses, Christians both tell of their own experience and also pass on a message which comes from God himself, is borne by Jesus to the world, and lives on in his Church.

This idea is suggested by the repeated use of the word 'servant'. The readers of the book are God's servants, as is John, through whom the message comes. The word translated 'servant' literally means slave, and some object to it as giving too servile a view of Christian discipleship. But that is to miss the point. In the Greek Bible with which many of John's readers would be familiar, 'slave of God' translates a Hebrew phrase meaning 'servant of the Lord' which is frequently used of the prophets. It is a term of honour, denoting those servants of the king who have been brought into his confidence and share a knowledge of his plans (see, for instance, Amos 3:7: 'Surely the Lord does nothing, without revealing his secret to his servants the prophets.') So the servants of God are those who know God's plans and proclaim them to the world.

Hearers

To pass on the message, though, we need to be hearers of it. John's opening verses include a blessing on the one who reads it out, and thus shares its message, and on those who hear and take to heart its teaching. This is not simply a pious wish. Communicating the word brings a share in the work of God and his prophetic message. To be open to the word of God is to let him into our lives, to get to know him, and to learn how to serve him. John refers only to his own book of prophecy, but it is true of all the Bible. As we read, reflect and pray, we can expect to be blessed; blessed by a deeper knowledge, but also by a deeper experience of the God who speaks to us, fills us with his message, and sends us out to speak good news to the world.

PRAYER

Father, as you speak to us through your word, give us grace to understand it, to live by it and to share it with others.

2

Postmarked heaven

John now writes a second introduction because, while the book is a prophecy in the style of an apocalypse, it is also in the form of a letter. It is a personal communication from John, who wants to share his vision and reflection with the churches for which he cares so deeply. In the New Testament, letters are the common way of bringing pastoral advice, and Revelation is intended as a pastoral letter.

These verses follow what was by now a well-established way of writing a Christian letter. Like most letters of the ancient world, it begins by stating who it is from, and who it is written to. Pagan writers would often follow this simple address with a brief blessing or prayer to one of the gods. Christians tended to extend this section into a lengthy thanksgiving or a hymn of praise to God (look at the way Paul begins his letters).

This letter comes with a wish of grace (God's free giving of his love and salvation) and the peace it brings, both with God and in the inner self. This wish is no mere formality. It is rooted in the nature and work of God himself. It comes from the eternal and unchanging God, the Lord of past, present and future. It comes from the Holy Spirit, here called the seven spirits before the throne of God. The number seven signifies perfection, but it also ties in with the seven churches—the Holy Spirit is the presence of God with the churches. Grace and peace come also from Jesus Christ, who because he was faithful to God, has been raised from the dead as the forerunner of all who will share in his resurrection, and who is now the true ruler of the world.

Three in one

We often hear that the doctrine of the holy Trinity is not found in the Bible. In the sense of the philosophical statements which later theologians loved this is true. But here, and often in Revelation, we see the close connection of Father, Son and Spirit, ruler/creator, saviour and indwelling presence, which is the foundation of the later trinitarian doctrines. If the Trinity is not found in a clearly formulated way in the New Testament, it is nevertheless the most thoroughly biblical way of speaking of God.

The glory of the Church, the glory of Christ

Although Revelation has much to say about heaven and future hope, it has as much, if not more, to say about the Church on earth. Christians have been called to be God's own people here and now. We have the task of approaching God in worship and bringing others into his presence. Or as John puts it in his deliberately 'biblical' language, drawn from the Old Testament (Exodus 19:6) and from Christian tradition (compare 1 Peter 2:9), we are God's kingdom and his priests, because of what Jesus has done for us.

What Jesus has done is the expression of love. Revelation does not mention the love of God all that often. In fact, many condemn the book as falling far short of the true Christian ideal of love. So don't forget that here at the outset we are told that all the work of Christ flows from love, and that love was such that it led Jesus to die for us.

This Jesus who died is the one who in the end will rule all things in glory. If his reign is hidden now, there will be a time when it will be clear to all, and those who killed him (that is, all whose sins led him to the cross) will wail, or mourn over him (verse 7, combining Daniel 7:13 and Zechariah 12:10).

There are two ways of taking this statement. It could mean that they will wail in terror at judgment. But it could also mean that they will mourn in repentance for their sins. Probably John is deliberately ambiguous here, for as we shall see, both possibilities remain open.

PRAYER

Father, Son and Holy Spirit, help us to serve you, to worship you and to love you with all our hearts.

3 Overwhelming vision

John received his vision on the island of Patmos, about 65 miles from Ephesus. He was there, he says, on account of God's word and the testimony of Jesus. Probably, then, he was in exile for his public proclamation of the gospel. Such a punishment was generally reserved for highly-placed citizens who were likely to cause embarrassment, and it is possible that John was a prominent person in his home town, though we cannot be sure of this.

Nor can we be sure whether John was still on the island when he wrote his letter/book, since his mention of Patmos (verse 9) is in the past tense. What is certain is that Revelation is not simply an account of a vision or series of visions. It is shot through with careful and clever references to scripture and other religious writings of the day, it has a very careful though complex structure, and is obviously the result of deep reflection. Yet we need not doubt that a visionary experience underlay it, a vision or visions received while John was 'in the spirit', which probably suggests a trance. Nor need we doubt that it was a vision, or series of visions, of enough power and importance to convince John that he had the basis for a much needed message to his churches.

Bible pictures

John's vision came to him on the Lord's day, which probably means Sunday, the day on which Christians worshipped in celebration of the day of Jesus' resurrection. And it was Jesus that he saw.

This was no vision of the carpenter from Nazareth. Nor was it the Christ of the resurrection appearances, displaying the wounds of the cross. This is a figure of awe, and almost terror. The description, like most of the visions of Revelation, is not a literal picture of what, if anything, John really saw. In fact, as the history of art shows us, it is almost impossible to make an accurate drawing of many of John's visions. They are literary 'pictures' depending on the force of the words, and the meanings conjured up by their references to the Bible.

So John sees one like a 'Son of Man', a reference to the figure in Daniel 7:13 who represents the people of Israel. This Son of man, though, has white hair and clothes, like Daniel's 'Ancient of Days'—God himself (Daniel 7:9)—and like God himself, can be described as the first and the last (see 1:8, where God is called Alpha and Omega—the first and last letters of the Greek alphabet). He wears the girdle of a high priest and from his mouth comes a sword, which can only be the word of God (see Hebrews 4:12). His face shines like that of Moses after meeting with God (Exodus 34:12).

So we can see how John weaves together various biblical images to give a picture of the power of the ascended Christ. Jesus, says John, stands as the representative of God's people, interceding for them and offering sacrifice like the Jewish high priest, but with greater effectiveness, for he shares the nature of God. Like Moses, he speaks God's word, which is his weapon against falsehood and evil, and he shines with the glory of God.

It is not surprising that John should fall down at the feet of this apparition. But Jesus comes to bring not fear, but hope, and victory over death.

Even this awesome image is not all that John has to tell us about Jesus, but it is enough for now. The One whose thunderous voice speaks through John to the churches is a figure of power, and he offers both hope and challenge. Yet he is not, for all his awesomeness, a distant figure. The stars in his hand, and the lampstands among which he stands represent the seven churches; and in their turn these churches represent all churches, for seven is the number of completion and fulness. Jesus has the Church in his hand, and stands amongst his people. He may sometimes have harsh words to say, but in the end, he is on their side, and his power is for them.

PRAYER

Lord, give us a vision of your glory, that we may draw on your strength for the tasks you give us to do.

4 The holder of eternal life

Like a play within a play, John gives us seven letters within his letter. Perhaps they are better called 'messages' since they lack some of the normal signs of a formal letter. They are addressed to seven churches in the Roman province of Asia, roughly what we would now call Turkey. We know that there were more than seven churches in the province (Colossae, for example, was not far away), and it may be that John is writing only to the Christian communities where he was well known, or where there were particular problems to be dealt with. We should not forget that Revelation is itself a letter, and so had a pastoral purpose, like the other letters of the New Testament.

On the other hand, we have already seen that seven is a symbolic number, suggesting a message for all the Church, and perhaps for all the churches in Asia, with a special address to certain problem communities.

The order in which the churches are named follows the route a messenger would take in a roughly circular journey from Ephesus along the roads of the day. Presumably each church would receive its own copy, which was expected to be read aloud to the congregation (1:3) at its meeting for worship. Such a setting would reinforce the impact of the book, with its interludes of praise and adoration.

The fact that it was to be read aloud also helps us to understand the structure of Revelation, with repeated variations on a particular phrase, three series of seven visions, and so on. These act as markers to the listeners, keeping their attention and helping them to make sense of a letter which would take over an hour to read.

Spiritual realities

Each message is addressed to 'the angel' of each church. There has been a lot of debate about the identity of these angels. Are they the guardian angels of each church? And if so, why should John write to them? And in what sense could a letter be addressed to an actual angel? Are they simply human representatives of each church, for the word literally means 'messengers'? And if so, why should Christ address only them when the whole Church is expected to listen? The best explanation is that they are heavenly beings who are in turn symbolic, representing the spiritual nature of the churches.

A church is not just a physical thing, either a building or even a collection of worshippers, but is a spiritual reality, a community of those with a shared faith, a shared experience of God, and a share in the Holy Spirit. John is told to write to the churches as spiritual entities, whose spiritual life is in fact in danger, whether their outward appearance is healthy or not.

So Jesus appears in John's first vision both standing among the lampstands which represent the churches, and holding in his hand the seven stars which are the spiritual life of the churches. Ultimately, it is this spiritual life which matters, for it is that which lasts for eternity.

Stars

That stars are used to represent the eternal life of the Church is probably a dig at the role astrology played in the ancient world, both as a means of telling the future (which is still with us in a big way), and in pagan religious symbolism. For many in the ancient world, life was governed by an inescapable fate. The sensible person simply accepted what came. John certainly does not share this view. For Christians both future and spiritual security are found in Jesus. God alone rules our destiny, and with that knowledge we do not need to know what is to come, save to be sure that he will be there waiting for us.

PRAYER

Lord Jesus, in you alone are we secure, and in you alone we put our trust.

5 Ephesus—love and doctrine

Ephesus was one of the major cities of the Roman province of Asia, along with Smyrna, and the capital, Pergamum. The town was a prosperous port and trading centre, dominated by the great temple of Artemis, which was known as one of the wonders of the ancient world. Paul had evangelized there, and fallen foul of both local religion and trade interests (Acts 19:23–41). In the midst of such a city, it would be easy for Christians to be led astray, but to their credit, the Ephesian Christians had stood firm.

True doctrine

In fact, it would seem that they had become very zealous in their defence of right doctrine. They had carefully evaluated visiting Christian teachers, and rejected their claim to be apostles. They opposed the activities of the Nicolaitans, a group which we will consider in more detail later. In the face of pressure to give up on their faith, they showed patience and endurance. And all this is commendable.

In fact, a high regard for doctrine is vital to the life of the Church. Without it, there can be no test of conformity with basic Christian teaching, and no check on what actually constitutes Christianity itself. Indeed, false teaching which would pervert the true gospel was an expected sign of the end times (Matthew 24:24; 1 John 2:18ff).

Yet the Ephesians' regard for sound teaching carried with it its own danger, and one into which the church had fallen. They had lost love, and so fallen foul of one of the other expected signs of the end (Matthew 24:12).

Had they become judgmental, and unyielding? Quite possibly.

Any community which feels itself under threat tends to tighten its rules and become less tolerant of dissent, and the Church is no exception. In our own time, we can see trends which look to touchstones of orthodoxy (as defined by each differing group) and which lead to condemnation of those who differ. There is a fine line to tread between holding to the faith and accepting those of different opinion, but if there is a choice to be made, it is better to err on the side of love.

So the church of Ephesus has fallen and is called to repent. Perhaps their description as fallen carries a reminder of Isaiah 14:12: 'How you are fallen from heaven, O Day Star, son of Dawn!' The star which is the church of Ephesus has plunged into the depths of lovelessness and must return to its former love or die. The verse from Isaiah was seen as a reference to the fall of the devil, and like Satan himself, the Ephesian church had lost the sign of God's grace.

Church of death

Christ's threat to come and remove their lampstand (that is, the church itself—1:20) is probably not a reference to his coming at the final judgment, though it may well include that. The threat is much more immediate. Churches do die, though the universal Church is eternal. And the surest route to death is to lose love.

For all its doctrinal uprightness (and, probably, fierce moral rectitude, for these tend to go together), there would be little welcome extended by the Ephesian church. Little concern for the needs of its neighbours, and little support for the weak within the church. None of this is a recipe for life and growth.

The task of the church then, was to hold fast to the faith by all means, but never to lose sight of the greatest of the commandments, to love. Love, after all, is the clearest sign of living faith.

PRAYER

Father, give us grace to discern your truth, perseverance to hold to it, but above all, give us love for you, for our sisters and brothers in Christ, and for the world in which we . are called to serve you.

6 Smyrna—poverty and riches

Smyrna (the modern town of Izmir) lay 35 miles north of Ephesus and vied with it for pre-eminence in trade and political influence. After its destruction in war, it had been rebuilt in 290BC as a model city and was famed for the beauty and grandeur of its buildings. It was an important centre for the worship of the emperor, and housed a large Jewish community.

In contrast, the Christian community was poor and persecuted. It is worth noting that only two of the seven churches (the other is Philadelphia) receive unqualified praise from the risen Christ, and both of these are noted for their poverty. The spiritual danger of material wealth, which is all too easily mistaken for divine blessing, was a reality then as now.

Yet the poverty of the Smyrnan Christians is more than offset by their spiritual wealth. In the Bible, while poverty is never seen as a virtue in itself, it is frequently connected with God's blessing, for the poor have nowhere to turn but to God, and so become a byword for simple trust.

Witnesses

The Christians of Smyrna are facing persecution by their more prosperous Jewish neighbours, probably in the form of denunciation to the Roman authorities as members of an anti-imperial cult. Some will be imprisoned for a short time ('ten days' merely indicates a short time), as a prelude, probably, to death. So they must hold firm to their faith, and be prepared to witness to the reality of Jesus by their deaths.

The Greek word for witness, *martys*, gives us the term, martyr—one whose witness has been taken to its ultimate conclusion. Revelation comes close to using the word in its modern sense, for all Christians, says John, must be prepared to die for their faith, if that is what is demanded of them.

The result of faithful witness is eternal life, which is the crown of victory given to the conquering faithful. So this message comes to Smyrna from the one who himself 'was dead and came to life'. The way of discipleship follows the path of Jesus to the cross, and beyond it to deathless life.

Most of the readers of this commentary do not expect to face any real danger for their faith, so it is difficult for us to remember that martyrdom is demanded of many of our brothers and sisters in Christ. It has been said that the twentieth century has seen more Christians martyred than all the rest of the Church's history. It is a salutary reminder that for Christians, the worst that can happen is not death, but the loss of eternal life.

Satan's synagogue

John's description of the Jews of Smyrna as the synagogue of Satan, who are not true Jews at all, is one that sits uneasily in our properly sensitive consciences. We have seen too much of the results of anti-Semitism to be easy with such terms. Yet for John, the situation was different. Christians were beginning to break with Judaism, and to be expelled from the Jewish community. For many Jewish Christians it was a loss of friends, family and identity. It was also a loss of protection, for Jews alone were exempt from the requirements of Roman civil religion, with its demands of worship offered to the gods of Rome and to the emperor himself.

For Jews to denounce those who like themselves shared a fierce loyalty to the one God of the Hebrew scriptures was to behave in a most un-Jewish way. Surely these were not true Jews, but had fallen prey to the devil himself!

PRAYER

Lord Jesus, when we must speak for you, give us courage.

7

Pergamum—the devil's capital

By now, it is fairly clear that the description of Christ which begins each of the messages to the seven churches is taken from John's first vision in 1:12–20. Each aspect of that vision ties in with some aspect of the situation of the seven churches. So far we have seen the fallen star of Ephesus and the resurrection promise to Smyrna. Pergamum, the provincial capital, is addressed by the one who 'has the sharp two-edged sword'. Roman provincial governors had the power of summary execution, the *ius gladii*, the right to use the sword. But the true ruler of the world is Jesus, whose word cuts not the body, but the soul, and the binding power of sin.

Each of the seven messages begins with a connection to the first chapter of Revelation in its description of Jesus, and ends with a promise to 'whoever conquers' which looks forward to the end of the book (chapters 21–22). The nature of the Christian's conquest is the theme of the book as a whole, while the reward of that victory is the tree of life, freedom from the second death, and so on.

This means that the seven messages cannot be dealt with fairly if they are taken out of their context as part of the whole book. At one time many scholars tried to do this, suggesting that they were earlier epistles which had been stuck into the book to give it greater relevance. Very few experts believe this now, but preachers still fall into the trap!

Heart of evil

Pergamum is not only the capital of Asia, it is Satan's home. There are many reasons why this was an apt description. The city was the site of a great temple to Zeus (whose magnificent altar, with a frieze showing the battle of the Greek gods against the earth giants can be seen in the Pergamon Museum in Berlin). It was also the centre of worship of the healing god, Asklepios, 'god of Pergamum'. To Christians the worship of these deities was not simply ignorance or folly, but was worship offered to demons (1 Corinthians 10:20).

But the best reason for the title was that Pergamum was the prime centre of the emperor cult. It housed a temple dedicated in his lifetime to the emperor Augustus, and to Roma, the goddess who was the personification of Rome. Technically, the emperor was not worshipped; prayer was offered to his *genius*, or guiding spirit, though in the eastern empire that distinction was rarely made, as there was already a tradition of divine kingship in eastern thought. For that matter, many emperors disliked the practice, but few discouraged it, and some revelled in the honour. Certainly, Domitian, emperor at the time of John's writing, liked to be addressed as 'Lord and God'. This was a title that Christians could not in conscience use.

Quite possibly that is how Antipas met his end. We are told nothing of this martyr, save that his death was part of a time of intense pressure on the church, a pressure which the church has successfully resisted.

Resisting the devil

Whether it was the lure of a pure church, leading away from love in Ephesus, the persecution of the church by those who should know better in Smyrna or the pressure of paganism at Pergamum, the church was under threat. In each case, that threat is seen as being the devil's work, and is something to be identified and resisted.

In our sophisticated age, belief in the devil seems old-fashioned, and indeed such a belief is not an article of the creeds. (The force of evil can readily be seen embedded in unjust laws, human institutions and the like.) All the same, it is vital to realize that the Church faces active opposition, for which the term 'demonic' seems fitting. At Pergamum and throughout Revelation that opposition is mainly from a state which demands more of its subjects than is its due. We today need to identify the opposing power and be aware of the need to resist.

PRAYER

Open our eyes, Lord, to that which opposes you, and help us resist.

8 Good neighbours or witnesses?

The church of Pergamum has so far stood firm against the direct attacks of Satan's city. Yet there is another danger which is not so obvious, for it comes from within.

There are some members of the church who are described as holding the teaching of Balaam. In the Old Testament, Balaam is a rather ambiguous character, a non-Israelite prophet who was hired by Balak, the king of Moab, to curse the invading Israelites. Under God's influence, he was able only to give blessings (Numbers 22–24). However, he was later credited with leading the Israelites astray so that they joined in the fertility cults of Moab, committing adultery with Moabite women, and worshipping their gods (Numbers 31:16). So he became a byword for those who would lead Israel astray.

Linked with the 'Balaamites' is another group, the Nicolaitans, presumably followers of someone called Nicolaus, of whom we know nothing, save that both groups seem to have had much the same sort of ideas. But what were those ideas?

Living in the pagan world

Since Balaam was said to have incited the Israelites to join in with the pagan practices they discovered in Moab, it seems reasonable to assume that something of the sort was going on in Pergamum. We know from elsewhere in the New Testament that some Christians felt that their Spirit-filled lives gave them immunity from the consequences of sin. The Corinthians argued that sexual promiscuity was irrelevant both to their lives and to Christ, and could be indulged in without harm (1 Corinthians 6:12–20). Similarly in Corinth there were those who said that meat which had been used in pagan sacrifices was harmless for Christian consumption; a view Paul agreed with, but which other Christians could not accept (1 Corinthians 8–10). Food sacrificed to idols had been forbidden by the church in Jerusalem in its decree to Gentile converts (Acts 15; 20:29).

Later forms of 'gnostic' Christianity (which saw salvation as the possession of spiritual knowledge) took a view similar to the Corinthians, and pursued it to extremes. So it seems likely that in Pergamum, and as we shall see, in other churches in Asia, a similar situation had arisen.

For Christians, avoiding contact with paganism could be tantamount to social ostracism. Social, political and business life centred on the worship of pagan gods. Meals were eaten in their temples, trade guilds had patron deities, and over all was the cult of the emperor, a binding force of political conformity. Christians could lose social prestige, friendship and wealth. Why not, then, make an outward show of conformity? Christ was the one true Lord, there was only one true God, so what harm was there in making a show for form's sake?

Fitting in

We can sympathize with a view like that, for though being a Christian carries lesser dangers in the modern Western world, few Christians like to be seen as odd or unsociable. Yet the real danger, then and now, is twofold.

Firstly, conformity with the world, can, if we are not careful, lead to a habit of acquiescence in things that really do matter.

Secondly, and more importantly, such deadly conformity robs the Church of effective witness. An outward show of pagan worship would simply send the message that Christ is but one of the teeming multitude of deities, with no greater claim than any other. Such a message is a far cry from the gospel the Church is called to proclaim.

For us, perhaps the danger is of suggesting that Christianity is merely one lifestyle or philosophy among many. It is 'all right for those who like that sort of thing'. In first-century Pergamum or in modern Manchester, such a message is a denial of Jesus and his claims.

PRAYER

Lord, give us wisdom to see where to draw the line, and when it is necessary, courage to stand up for you.

9

A new name

If we are right in seeing the false teaching at Pergamum as conformity with the world, the next verse is rather worrying. The Pergamene Christians are called to repent. To many modern readers, their stance may not seem all that sinful. Yet this is one of the main themes of Revelation. The world in which Christians are called to live out their discipleship is not a neutral territory. It is one pervaded by attitudes, social and political systems, which add up to hostility towards God.

The church at Pergamum is so far holding fast, and showing courage in doing so. Yet from within comes a teaching which may soften resolve and kill the church more effectively than any persecution. And of course, the fornication of verse 14 could well be literal. Some of the Pergamenes, like the Corinthians before them, could well have been much more enthusiastic partakers in certain aspects of pagan worship than a mere show of conformity called for!

The whole church is therefore called to repent. Accepting some who differ in opinion may well be commendable tolerance. But failure to show up the dangers of their arguments and practices is another matter. So Christ threatens to use the sword of his mouth—compromise may have helped them avoid the Roman sword, but the judgment of God is unavoidable.

The Spirit of prophecy

Like all the messages to the seven churches, this is a prophecy for all the churches. The problem may be at its most severe in Pergamum (and Thyatira, as we shall see) but it is a perennial danger.

The message comes from the Spirit of God, whose task is to communicate God's will to his Church. The task of the Church, in its turn, is to listen to what God is saying. All too often, the Church pursues its own, apparently reasonable, agenda. But that does not mean that it is obeying God.

To stress the role of the Spirit, John uses two terms. In 1:4, the Holy Spirit is described as the seven spirits before God's throne, stressing the Spirit as the indwelling power of God for the seven (and all) churches. Elsewhere John prefers the more usual 'Spirit of God', the Old Testament term for the one who inspires the prophets. The Holy Spirit is both indwelling life and the bringer of God's word.

A new name

Again, Christ's message ends with a promise to those who conquer. They will receive the hidden manna. According to Jewish tradition, in the end times, God would again feed his people on manna in the age of the Messiah. For Christians this has already come true in the giving of Jesus, the bread for the life of the world (John 6:31–35, 58), and was celebrated in the eucharist. Ultimately, that spiritual sustenance will be theirs for all eternity.

They will also be given a new name, inscribed on a white stone. Both of these images are obscure, and several interpretations have been suggested. White stones were used as admission tickets to banquets and as signs of acquittal at trials. The name may be that of Christ but as that promise is given to the church of Philadelphia (3:12), it is more likely to be a new name for the individual. This denotes a new identity, since in John's day, people's names were held to encapsulate their personalities, their 'true selves'.

Victorious Christians will find their true selves in their relationship with Jesus, and will be acquitted at the last judgment, gaining entrance to the marriage feast of their Lord, of which the present eucharist is but a foretaste.

PRAYER

Lord, as we feed on you now, make us hungry for your word, hungry to do your will, and hungry for you.

10

The growing church

Thyatira was the politically least important of the seven cities, but its church receives the longest letter. Its central place in the seven messages may well suggest that its problems were well known. Certainly verse 23 suggests that Christ's response to the church will be a lesson for all the churches.

Despite the stern warning Jesus has for the Thyatiran Christians, their church has much in its favour. Its life is developing, and the signs of the Spirit's work (see Galatians 5:22f) are abundant.

We tend to think of spiritual growth as being something that applies only to individuals. The seven messages to the Asian churches remind us that growth is necessary to churches as well. The Ephesian church grew in zeal for doctrine, but that was a lop-sided growth which needed to be balanced by a growth in love. At Thyatira, there has been an increase in love, and in faith which in Revelation tends to mean faithfulness. Christian faith is not just about believing a set of doctrines, but about having trust in another person—God.

Similarly love is no mere sentiment, but shows itself in service. We are not told whether this is service to God or to fellow Christians, but it is unlikely that John would make that distinction. To serve Christ is to serve others.

It would be nice to think that a community which was visibly growing in love and service would gain the respect of its neighbours, but the world is rarely so fair. So patient endurance is another necessary virtue. We are not explicitly told what problems the Thyatirans faced, but on the evidence of Smyrna and Pergamum, it seems likely that some sort of persecution was in mind, though not so violent as to need special mention. Quite possibly it took the form of social ostracism, or at least avoidance of Christians by their pagan neighbours.

They need no more than they already have, and their Lord does not lay on them any further burden (verse 24).

Jezebel

Yet the use of the phrase, 'any other burden' recalls the language of the apostolic decree of Acts 15:28, which forbade, among other things, the eating of food offered to idols. Eating such food is one of the things encouraged by Jezebel, who is the fly in the ointment at Thyatira. The name is obviously John's nickname for this prophet who is leading the flock astray (elsewhere in Revelation, the word translated 'beguiling' is used only of Satan and his minions).

Jezebel, the pagan wife of king Ahab of Israel, was legendary as a perverter of the faith of Israel. The daughter of the king of Damascus, she was a keen promoter of her own faith in the fertility god Baal. She was accused of 'many whoredoms and sorceries' (2 Kings 9:22), a reference more to the fertility rites of Baal than to her own behaviour, though this did not stop short of arranging murder (1 Kings 21:1–16).

Prophet v. prophet

Jezebel 'calls herself a prophet' and was no doubt accepted as such in the church of Thyatira. This was the problem. What do we do when two prophets disagree? Both claim the inspiration of the Holy Spirit, and both may offer words which sound, on the face of it, quite reasonable. Yet to the prophet John, Jezebel is a deceiver who is virtually in league with the devil.

It was an old problem with no easy solution, save that of 'wait and see', as in the confrontation between the prophets Jeremiah and Hananiah—Jeremiah 28. John in fact takes a similar line: Jezebel and her followers will not last long (verses 22f).

PRAYER

Lord give grace to your Church to grow in love, faith, service and endurance; and discernment to recognize your voice out of all the clamour of the world.

Trusting in God

The prophet Jezebel is leading astray some of the Thyatiran Christians. But into what? Thyatira was an active centre of commerce, dominated by its merchants and the trade guilds to which they belonged. (Lydia, the seller of purple cloth in Acts 16 was a Thyatiran.) So numerous and influential were these guilds that the archeology of Thyatira provides us with most of our information on such guilds for this period.

The guilds were dedicated to various pagan gods, who functioned much like patron saints. Guild business and social life would be centred on the appropriate temple. In practice, this probably meant little more to most guild members than dinner in a favourite restaurant would to modern business people. Yet the fact remained that guilds were run under the auspices of what to Christians were idolatrous cults. Their meals were the results of pagan sacrifices, and their business agreements were in the name of false gods. Could Christians take part in such things?

Refusal to do so could mean ruin and ostracism. Compliance could be seen as denial of Christ. Since Jezebel encouraged the eating of food offered to idols, it seems likely that she, like the Balaamites of Pergamum and the Nicolaitans, saw no harm in Christian involvement in such bland worship. She could probably cite Paul, who agreed that food offered to idols was mainly a matter of individual conscience (1 Corinthians 8:4ff). Yet Paul knew there were spiritual dangers involved (1 Corinthians 10:14ff). There is no hint of such a concern with Jezebel.

Deep dangers

If this were all, then John's strong attack may be understandable, as one who disagreed, but we may well feel more sympathetic with his target. However, there are hints that there is more going on. The reference to the 'deep things' and to the promised star suggest that gnosticism and astrology are in view. This may be all the more likely when we remember the original Jezebel's 'sorceries'.

Gnosticism (from *gnosis*—the Greek for knowledge) was a religious tradition which claimed that salvation came from secret knowledge given by God to those who were worthy of it. Gnostics claimed to know the 'deep things of God'. Such knowledge set them free from the ordinary world, and gave them spiritual protection, so that they could encounter evil without succumbing to it. Such teaching found a fertile ground in Christianity, with its apparently similar stress on spiritual freedom and the teaching of Jesus. The great difference was that Christianity presented an open call to receive God's grace in Christ; gnosticism presented a secret knowledge.

For John, this is a denial of the gospel, and the deep things are deep things of Satan.

Exploring evil

On the other hand, it may be Jezebel's own term. For some gnostics, their spiritual protection enabled them to indulge in immorality and idolatry with impunity. While Jezebel's 'fornication' is a standard metaphor for idolatry and false teaching, it could also be literal, as it was for some Corinthians (1 Corinthians 6:12–20). Perhaps some of Jezebel's followers plunged into sinful activities (quite easy at some guild banquets, which could become pretty wild affairs) believing themselves to be spiritually protected.

A similar attitude may have been held towards the astrology which was so much a part of the ancient world, and which would be consulted by prudent traders. For Christians, though, the future is held in God's hands, and he alone controls it. Reliance on the stars is a denial of trust in the true Lord of the future.

PRAYER

Lord, help us to trust only you, for the future and for the present, and to rely on your grace alone.

12 Judgment and victory

The risen Christ has given Jezebel time to repent. We are not told how, but it may well be that John has had a brush with her before, and she has continued in her teaching. Now the time of reckoning is approaching. Those who have committed adultery with her will suffer great distress and her children will be struck dead (literally, 'will be killed with death', 'death' here having its other Greek meaning of pestilence). Probably we should see two groups here: those who have flirted with her teaching but are not fully committed; and a distinct group in the church of Thyatira which is committed to Jezebel's leadership. Jezebel herself will be thrown on a bed (an obvious double meaning).

In a book as full of symbolism as Revelation, we need not take this threat too literally (but see 1 Corinthians 11:30). Whatever John envisages, the time is short for the false teachers of Thyatira.

Together with all the other churches, Thyatira must be prepared for persecution, and in that time, only a strong and distinct Christian faith will survive. Compromise will be no protection, and a faith that has been watered down will lack the strength necessary for survival. Now is the time to repent, and to learn to trust in God alone.

Holding fast

Thus the task of the Church is to cling to what it knows to be true, the teaching passed on to it by the apostles, and to the growth in faith and love which that has brought. Above all, what it has is Christ, and he is worth all that it may gain by compromise with the world, and more. The path to final victory is faithfulness to Christ.

So this church too receives a promise, to share in the final rule of Jesus over the nations. The word translated 'rule' literally means to shepherd, and there is a double meaning here. The promise quotes Psalm 2:9, which is prepared for by the description of Jesus as Son of God in 3:18 (the only time in Revelation) which is also a reference to this messianic Psalm (Psalm 2:7). In the psalm the iron rod or sceptre is the instrument of judgment and conquest, shattering the pride of the world like clay pots. Yet it can also be the shepherd's staff of protection and guidance. Then the clay pots are broken that they might be remoulded, as in Jeremiah 18:1–11. As in 1:7 the coming judgment of Christ may be salvation or doom. Either way, the Church must be firm in its witness, and uncompromising in its devotion to Jesus. Indeed, it is only through such witness that there is hope of salvation for the nations. If Christ's own people are seen not to bother too much about loyalty to him, how can those who do not believe be expected to turn to him? If the Church is not seen to repent of its sins, how can it call the world to repentance?

In this sense, authority over the nations does not wait for the end of time. By faithfulness to Christ, moral uprightness, and loyal witness, the Church is called to exercise moral authority here and now. Its very existence should be a statement of an alternative and greater authority. The question for today is still one of compromise. Is there anything in the Church and in Christian living which truly distinguishes it from the world? John's call to hear what the Spirit is saying to the churches is still pertinent.

Star of glory

Venus, the brightest of the stars, was associated with victory and rulership. For those who abandoned their trust in the stars, the true ruler and victor would be theirs—Jesus himself, the brightest star in heaven (22:16). Again, the message to the local church looks forward to the end of the book. Indeed, there have been hints throughout the letter to Thyatira of what is coming. Jezebel is described in terms reminiscent of the whore who is Rome/Babylon (chapter 17), while harlots and sorcerers are excluded from the New Jerusalem in 21:8.

PRAYER

Lord, give your Church strength to be different, and discernment to know where difference is called for.

13 Church of the living dead

The city of Sardis had once been the capital of Croesus, king of Lydia, fabled for his wealth. Now its fortunes were in decline. Its mighty fortress was impregnable—except that it was now deserted, and had fallen twice to enemies who had crept up on it secretly. In John's day Sardis boasted a temple to the mother goddess Cybele, and a powerful Jewish community. Either of these interest groups might have been expected to oppose the Christian church in their city. Yet there is not the slightest hint of persecution or opposition in this fifth message. The reason is that the church is dead.

It has not been wiped out, nor has it died from lack of interest. To outside eyes this is a lively and vibrant church, with a reputation. Yet from God's point of view death reigns in Sardis. The reason for that death is that Christ has not found their works 'perfect'. This does not mean flawless, but literally, 'completed' or 'fulfilled'. In complete contrast to Thyatira, whose works have grown to maturity, the start made at Sardis has come to nothing. To be sure, there is still a church there. But it does nothing. There has been no opposition to Christianity in Sardis, because Christianity is not being proclaimed. There is nothing but a harmless outer show.

Hollow church

We are not told exactly what was going on at Sardis, but we can make a good guess, for we have modern analogies. It is easy for a church to put on a show. Its services may be lively and enjoyable, they may be beautiful and apparently reverent. But the substance of the church's witness and spirituality can all the same be hollow. The church may be a fun place to visit, but it will offer no challenge to lives and morals, no call to repentance and no threat to anyone else. It will not face persecution, but it will not gain eternal life either.

This is the threat to the church at Sardis. The one who holds the spiritual life of the churches, the seven stars, and who gives the life-giving Holy Spirit (the seven spirits) is only too well aware of the lack of life there.

Like the city itself in times past, the church is unprepared for the surprise visit of its Lord (Matthew 24:42–51). Once again, this may refer to the Second Coming, but also to much sooner judgment, as the church eventually withers away.

Hope

Yet there is still hope. An ember of their first faith still glows, which may yet be rekindled. They are still aware of the teaching they first received. Some of the Christians have made a stand and tried to follow Christ wholeheartedly. If the church follows their example, being true to the call it received in baptism it may yet live. The white robes worn by the newly baptized will be an eternal sign of righteousness and new life. Jesus will proudly proclaim his followers to God the Father (Matthew 10:32f). The call is to be alert and watchful, active in witness and service.

The signs, though, are not good. As things stand, the church of Sardis will be blotted out of the book of life. To Greek citizens, this would suggest being struck off the register of citizens of the new Jerusalem. To Jews it would mean being removed from the list of those favoured by God. Either way, the message is stark. Repent or be doomed.

PRAYER

Lord, keep us awake and watchful. Keep us faithful and active. Do not let us fool ourselves with outward show, but enrich and nourish our inner lives, our witness and our service.

14

REVELATION 3:7-13
Faithful church

The next message is a far happier one. Like that to Smyrna, this letter carries no condemnation. Also like Smyrna, the church in Philadelphia is weak in the eyes of the world. Yet the 'little power' it has is bolstered by the love of God (verse 9), and it has been faithful to Jesus in the face of persecution by the local synagogue.

This message, then, comes from the one who is himself utterly trustworthy, the holy and true one. 'True' in Greek thinking meant 'real', while in Hebrew it carried the idea of trustworthiness. Both senses apply here. The trustworthy reality on which the church relies is found in Christ, who carries the authority of God himself, the Holy One of Israel.

Jesus, the trustworthy one, holds the future of the church, for he has the key of David. This is a reference to Isaiah 22:15–25 in which the ambitious royal steward, Shebna, is replaced by the trustworthy Eliakim. So Jesus replaces all that his followers have previously relied upon, and becomes the basis of their security. There is also a reference back to 1:18, for the risen Christ holds the keys of Death and Hades. The one who has conquered death through the resurrection has the power to overcome death, and unlock the realm of the dead for his followers.

Christians therefore need not fear even death itself, for to them it becomes the doorway to eternal life. That doorway stands open to the church at Philadelphia and their eternal destiny is secure, as long as they stand firm.

So far, they have indeed stood firm, loyal to the word of the gospel which they accepted. For them it has become a 'word of patient endurance' in the face of the 'synagogue of Satan'. Like the Smyrnan Christians, the church of Philadelphia has no doubt found itself exposed to Roman law by being expelled from the protection offered by the synagogue.

Trouble ahead

Trouble is by no means at an end. The church has been tested by its enemies, but now a time of trial faces the whole world as the judgment of God draws near. Jesus is coming, and his coming will be heralded by a time of tribulation.

The Jews had long held that the coming of the Messiah would bring a time of testing to the world, and Christians shared that view. Jesus promises his faithful followers that they will be preserved in this time.

In one way of looking at the book of Revelation which is common in fundamentalist circles, this is a promise that God will miraculously keep Christians safe from the afflictions which will strike unbelievers. Some even believe that God will remove Christians physically from the world so that they will not bear the full brunt of the time of trial. This view (the 'secret rapture') is based on 1 Thessalonians 4:17, where Paul is reassuring his converts that those who are still alive on the day of resurrection will not miss out on heaven. Paul certainly does not mean that they will miss out on tribulation, and there is no hint of such a view elsewhere in Revelation.

The best way to take 3:10 is a promise that Jesus will keep his followers firm in their faith and hope in the troubles which lie ahead. By holding firm, they are certain of their heavenly crown (verse 11).

PRAYER

Lord Jesus, hold us firmly when we are tempted to let you down in the face of persecution, mockery or lack of earthly support in our faith.

Pillars of the faith

The time of trouble which John foresees may on the face of it appear daunting. It will be a time of unrest and suffering for the world, and it will be a time of increased persecution of Christians, as we shall see later in the book. It is, though, a sign of hope. It means that Jesus is close, and the final vindication of the church is drawing near.

In the end, those who have persecuted the church will bow down and admit that their victims were right after all. The image of persecutors (here the Jews of Philadelphia are most clearly in view) bowing down is basically one of victory for the church. Yet there is some ambiguity. In the Old Testament, Israel is seen as finally being victorious over the nations, who will acknowledge both their defeat and the worthiness of the God of Israel. Israel will then become the nation which leads others to worship the true God (Isaiah 45:14; 60:14; Ezekiel 36:23). John reverses the Old Testament prophecy, for the unbelieving Jews who have rejected the Messiah will recognize him in the faith of the mainly Gentile Church. As we have noticed elsewhere, the final judgment still remains open, with the possibility of either salvation or condemnation for those who currently reject Christ.

Window of opportunity?

With this possibility in mind, there may well be a secondary meaning to the 'open door' Jesus has set before the church. The New Testament writers use this term to represent opportunity for preaching the gospel (Acts 14:27; 1 Corinthians 16:9; 2 Corinthians 2:12; Colossians 4:3). It is possible that John also has in mind the opportunity that lies before the church to proclaim the word of Christ, and so bring even their opponents to repentance. The main meaning though, is of the church's certain entry into the kingdom of God.

Even if there is no explicit reference to the church's witness in verse 8, it is vital to remember that this is one of the major tasks of the church. Indeed, in Revelation it is *the* task of the church.

Wherever opportunity presents itself, the Church is called to bear witness to Jesus, and to make opportunities as well!

Final destination

The concluding promise to the Philadelphian church is one that would strike chords of recognition. The church which is victorious will become a pillar in the temple of God. This takes up a common Christian theme, that the dwelling place of God is not a building, but his people, who are themselves his temple (1 Peter 2:5). Pillars are of course a symbol of strength and stability, often left standing when all else has fallen. This sight may well have been seen in Philadelphia a generation earlier when the city was rocked by an earthquake.

The city was rebuilt with imperial aid, and given the additional name, Neocaesarea in honour of the emperor. Christ's promise to give the name of New Jerusalem to his Church is a pertinent reminder that God is the one who rebuilds what is broken, and upholds what is steadfast. The Church will also bear the name of God and of Jesus, marked forever as his.

God of the poor

We have already seen that the two churches which receive unqualified praise are also notable for their poverty or powerlessness. Revelation is true to a major strand of biblical teaching which sees God as on the side of the poor and defenceless. If he is biased to the poor, then so should be the Church.

PRAYER

Father, thank you that you are biased. Thank you that you lean to mercy rather than judgment, and to the defenceless rather than the powerful.

16
Successful Christians?

The city of Laodicea was as fabled for its wealth as Sardis once had been. It was a banking centre specializing in currency exchange, it had a thriving clothing industry fed by the glossy black wool of the local sheep, and it housed a hospital and medical school well known for its eye treatments. At nearby Hieropolis were hot springs with reputed medicinal properties. All these provide the images for this, the most tragic of the seven messages to the churches. Even in the dead church of Sardis, there were some who followed Christ faithfully. Of Laodicea, Christ has nothing positive to say.

Lord of creation

The message comes from the one who is the Amen, another divine title applied to Jesus. In Isaiah 65:16 blessings and oaths are made in the name of the 'God of Amen'. The liturgical term 'amen' means 'so be it', and so NRSV translates Isaiah's phrase as 'God of faithfulness'. John can apply this title to Jesus because he is the 'faithful and true witness' who embodies God's steadfastness and trustworthiness. All that we need to know of God's love, saving power and promises to his people can be seen in Christ.

More even than this, Christ is the origin of creation, the one from and through whom all things come to be. The idea is expressed more fully in John 1:1–5, but the phrase used here is reminiscent of Colossians 1:15–20, a letter which was intended not only for Colossae but also for Laodicea (Colossians 4:16), and would be well known to the church there.

Speaking of Christ as the origin of creation is a way of saying that God's purposes of salvation are not a last ditch attempt to put things right, but are part of a plan which spans the whole of time. It is also a reminder that the world in which we live is God's and as such is the place where God is served. There is a perennial temptation for Christians to see their faith and worship as being about some 'spiritual' realm which has little or nothing to do with everyday life. If God is the creator, then creation is his area of activity, the object of his love, and the place where he is served. It is particularly important to keep this in mind when reading Revelation, for with its repeated visions of heaven and the future we may be tempted to forget that the purpose of the book is to inspire us to witness here and now.

Sickening church

The Laodiceans are neither hot nor cold. This is usually taken to be a reference to their spiritual zeal, and of course that is true. But it is their works which are in view. The church here is neither like the healing hot springs of neighbouring Hierapolis, nor the refreshing cold streams of nearby Colossae. It provides neither spiritual healing nor refreshment for the soul. It is like the waters of Hierapolis as they flow over the cliffs near Laodicea—tepid and laced with unpalatable minerals. The church is useless, and Jesus will spit it out. (The older translation, 'spew' gives the force of the term.)

The poor showing of the church is grounded in complacency. The Laodicean Christians share the wealth and prosperity of their city, and it is easy for them to look at their church as successful. Perhaps they even see their well-being as a sign of God's blessing. Certainly there is a misguided strand of thought amongst some modern Christians which mistakes material wealth for spiritual riches, and proclaims a 'gospel' which promises material success. Both the Laodiceans and their modern counterparts are about as wrong as you can get. In reality, they are pitiful in their spiritual poverty and blindness, and lie naked to the judgment of God.

PRAYER

Lord of creation, open our eyes to your truth, and inspire us to serve you and witness to you in the world you have made.

Love and glory

The Laodicean church is content to be a sharer in the riches of its native town. The sources of those riches have their spiritual counterparts, though, and in these they are completely lacking. So the message of the risen Lord comes to them: seek out a spiritual wealth which will resist the fire of judgment (see 1 Corinthians 3:13), righteousness which will cover their spiritual nakedness, and healing for spiritual blindness. For so far, they have shown nothing of the works which Christ demands of his church. Where is their witness to the truth of the gospel? Where is their challenge to the sins of the world? By silence and complacency they testify to the irrelevance of their faith.

Loving judge

The thoroughgoing condemnation of this church is delivered not in vindictiveness, but in love. There is still time to repent, and to become what they are called to be. If there were no hope, there would be no message. The message of condemnation is itself a sign of God's love, and of the distress they are causing to their Lord.

Indeed, it is to this, the least worthy of the seven churches that one of the most famous statements of God's love is delivered. Jesus stands at their door and knocks, waiting for them to hear and admit him. The one who has opened the door to heaven for the church of Sardis, now finds the door to the church of Laodicea shut in his face.

It will not always be this way. The one who knocks is the Lord of the Church, and he will gain admission. The question is, will he then invite his servants to join him for supper? The image of Jesus at the door recalls Jesus' parables of the bridegroom. In Luke 12:35–38 the master returns from the wedding banquet and invites those servants who are still alert to join him at the feast. In Matthew 25:1–13 the unready virgins find the door locked against them. The bridegroom has arrived, and they have missed the wedding supper. The Laodiceans have at present locked out Christ, but will discover that in truth they have locked themselves out of the kingdom of God.

Another allusion is to Song of Songs 5:2: 'I slept but my heart was awake. Listen! my beloved is knocking.' For Jews of John's time, this was interpreted allegorically as the searching of God for Israel. For the Laodiceans there is hope here. The bride is asleep, but her heart is awake. She can rouse from her slumber to meet the bridegroom. She must awaken before it is too late.

All these images which cling to the picture of Christ at the door reinforce the true motive of his condemnation. It is not the sentence of a legalistic judge, but the desperate plea of the rejected lover.

Final promise

Just as the greatest declaration of love is reserved for the most disappointing church, so the greatest promise is offered to it. The one who is victorious will share in the reign of Christ, seated with him on the throne.

It is a mistake to ask over whom they will reign. The point is that the promise to this church (and all the churches—verse 22) is that they will share in the life and glory of Christ himself. Salvation is about more than living forever in heaven. It is about the transformation of human existence in the presence of God. More than that we cannot really say, for 'what we will be has not yet been revealed. What we do know is this: when he is revealed, we will be like him, for we will see him as he is' (1 John 3:2).

PRAYER

Father, we do not know what you will finally make us in Christ, save that it will be the outworking of your love. Keep us firm in that love till then, that we may never lock you out, and may not be excluded ourselves.

18 God himself

After the initial greetings and challenges to the seven churches, the main body of John's book begins with an invitation from the risen Christ (the voice he had first heard—verse 1; cf. 1:10–13) to enter heaven itself. Revelation's understanding of heaven is not quite what we mean by the term. To us, heaven is the dwelling place of God, and the final destination of his people. In Revelation, it is where God is to be found, but it is itself a place where conflict occurs, and good and evil both exist for a time.

Perhaps the best way of expressing it is to say that heaven is seen as the realm of spiritual reality which underlies the world we see. Events in that realm affect what goes on on earth, and more surprisingly, heaven is affected by earthly events. In the final vision of God's triumph, both heaven and earth will be remade, and evil banished from both the physical and spiritual dimensions of creation.

By presenting this view of the spiritual realm, John reminds us that there are no actions without their spiritual consequences, and no spiritual experiences or beliefs which do not affect everyday life. John's vision of heaven is not a mystical flight from reality but a reminder of the hidden depths to everyday life and discipleship.

Indescribable God

The centre of heaven is a throne room, which will turn out also to be a temple. Several writers have pointed out that the description of the throne room reflects that of the Roman emperor. This does not mean that John sees God as simply a greater version of an earthly ruler. It is rather that he sees the pomp of earthly power as a vain attempt to mimic and usurp the rule of the true King. Compared to God's rule, though, the greatest king of earth is an insignificant pretender.

At the centre of heaven is the throne of God (Isaiah 6:1; Ezekiel 1:26). There is no real attempt to describe God. Instead, John writes in terms of precious stones, and stones whose very colour was highly variable. It is a vision of brilliance and richness, but beyond that words cannot go. While owing much to Ezekiel 1, which also speaks in terms of precious stones, John stops short of Ezekiel's vision of a human form (Ezekiel 1:26).

There are two reasons for John's reticence. Firstly, any attempt to describe God would fall short of reality, and come close to idolatry, for it would limit the power and majesty of the reality. Secondly, God is not a physical being, and John is aware of that fact. What he sees on the throne is no human or animal shape, but a presence which cannot be limited to physical terms. John is going out of his way to avoid the trap of anthropomorphism, for trying to describe him in human terms limits the limitless reality of God.

Some writers object that John still thinks of God in human terms, for he holds a scroll in his hand in 5:1 and elsewhere speaks out loud, but this misses the point. In speaking of God at all, we have to use imagery, and human imagery, while false, is still better than any other. What we must never lose sight of is that it *is* imagery. John sets this fact squarely in front of us at the outset.

Let God be God

If imagery is unavoidable it may seem silly to bother about it. However, the images we use govern the way we think. How often have we heard the phrase, 'I like to think of God as...?' The point of remembering the indescribable nature of God is that it stops us from fitting God into our own comfortable categories. Our task is not to confine God to the limits of our imaginations or desires, but to be open to what he wants to tell us about himself, about his will for us, and about ourselves. We need to let God set the agenda, and that is easier if we have no neat boxes into which we think we can fit him.

PRAYER

Father, keep me from the temptation of dictating to you, and instead let me learn from you.

19
Heaven and earth

The throne of God is surrounded by a jewelled rainbow. On the face of it, this is just one more trapping of magnificence, but its significance goes deeper than that. The rainbow was the sign of God's covenant with Noah (Genesis 9:13–17), his promise never again to destroy the inhabitants of the earth. As such it was the symbol of the mercy of God. If we try to visualize the picture John paints, we see God seated on a throne set against the backdrop not of his power, or his wrath or his judgment, but his mercy.

In all that follows, with the accounts of the dreadful judgment of God, we must keep this symbol in our minds. God is acting not out of a desire for vengeance or a delight in destruction, but in mercy. Exactly how judgment and mercy intermingle will be explained as the book unfolds.

Kingdom of priests

God's throne is not the only one. Twenty-four elders sit on their own thrones before God. Many commentators see these as angelic beings, the council of God (e.g. Job 2:1; Isaiah 6:2), but 'elders' is an unusual term for angels, so they are much more likely to be human beings.

There were twenty-four priestly families (1 Chronicles 14:4–6), and this leads some to see the elders as the Old Testament saints. However, while this offers a clue to their purpose, elsewhere in Revelation there is no particular interest in distinguishing the Old Testament people of God from the New. For John, there is one people of God, characterized by their faithful witness, be they saints of Old or New Testaments (see chapter 12). The number twenty-four is also reminiscent of the twelve patriarchs plus the twelve apostles, a combination which is later seen written on the walls of the new Jerusalem, which stands for the people of God (21:12–13). This is probably a better clue to their meaning. They stand for the whole of God's people. The elders offer worship, which ties in with their priestly role, while they also wear the crown of kingship. John has already described the Church as a kingdom of priests (1:6; cf.

Exodus 19:6; 1 Peter 1:9) and the crowned elders fit that idea. 'Kingdom' in biblical thought means not just a realm, but a kingly rule, so to be a kingdom can also mean a sharing in the rule of the kingdom. Here the representatives of God's people have become a part of his heavenly council.

Once again, as with the angels of the seven churches, John is reminding us that the reality of God's people is different from its earthly manifestation. On earth, both the Old and New Testament people may seem weak, sinful, persecuted or prone to failure. From the spiritual perspective, they are crowned servants of God.

You could say that the elders represent both how God counts his people and the destiny which awaits them. The present reality is different, as Jesus' witnesses await their vindication and final salvation (6:9–11).

The task of the Church is always to seek to make real in its present life something of the destiny which awaits; to become what we are. In that sense, the criticisms and commendations of the seven churches are based on the extent to which each church made manifest the kingdom of God in its own life. The same standard is, of course, that by which the Church of today is judged.

God of Sinai

The thunder and lightning are typical biblical trappings of God's presence, as at Mount Sinai (Exodus 19:16f). It provides a further reminder that the God of Christians is also the God of the Old Testament, and reflects the exodus symbolism which is so important to John.

PRAYER

Father, give grace to your people, that in our life and witness we may model the kingdom you have promised us, and so draw others into your rule.

20

REVELATION 4:5b–6a
Spirit of creation

The spirits we have already encountered are a symbol of the Holy Spirit (1:4). John's source for this image is Zechariah 4:2, 10 where seven lamps on a lampstand represent the 'eyes of God which range through the world'. The God who is at the centre of John's vision, and of his book, is the giver of the Spirit.

In Revelation, Zechariah's lampstand has become the seven stands which represent the seven churches (1:20). The lamps for the stands are the seven spirits. So John reminds us that the light, the vitality of the Church comes from the Holy Spirit who is God's gift to his people.

Creator God

At the same time, we need to remember that Zechariah's seven torches, the Spirit of God, range through the whole earth. God is the creator, and his Spirit is the Spirit of creation, and not just the possession of the Church. The Spirit stands before a crystal sea, which represents (amongst other things) the primal chaos out of which creation came and over which the Spirit of God hovered (Genesis 1:2).

Christians often need to be reminded that God is not active in the Church alone. To imagine otherwise is to limit the work of God and to foster an unbiblical division between the works of creation and redemption. The whole earth is the Lord's and he is at work in it. Often the task of the Church is to spot where God is at work in the world, and to take its cue from that.

Some Christians would argue, for instance, that joining forces with non-Christians who have a similar goal (such as social reform, or ecological awareness) is a betrayal of God. In fact, it is quite the opposite. It is an acknowledgment that he is to be served in all of his creation, and a recognition of the breadth of the Spirit's work. What is not acceptable, of course, is a watering down of the specifically Christian content of the Church's task and beliefs.

Sea of troubles

The crystal sea would also evoke a range of images in the minds of John's hearers. It would remind them of the Red Sea through which God brought his people to safety. It was seen as a metaphor for baptism (1 Corinthians 10:2) through which he still brings his people to safety. It could be patterned on the model sea in Solomon's temple (1 Kings 7:23–26) which was used for ritual washings (2 Chronicles 4:6).

Most of all, though, in the Bible, the sea is generally an image of destruction and of chaos. The crystal sea stands for the abyss from which evil comes, and over which God will triumph, for in the end, there will be no more sea (Revelation 21:1).

That there should be a symbol of chaos and evil in heaven may at first seem strange, but we should remember that heaven is the realm of spiritual reality, not the place of eternal blessedness. The crystal sea is part of the richness of John's picture of the spiritual realm, and reflects the New Testament conviction of spiritual as well as earthly evils (Ephesians 6:12). At the same time it is a symbol of God's deliverance of his people. Overall, then, we are presented with a picture of the merciful God who saves from the forces of chaos.

As the book develops we shall see in greater detail how spiritual evils translate into earthly, historic terms. What is becoming apparent even at this stage, though, is that in his visions of heaven, John is deeply concerned with the everyday life of the Church in the world.

PRAYER

Open our eyes, Lord, to the work of your Spirit in the world around us, that we may know where and how to serve you.

21 The song of creation

Completing the vision of the heavenly throne-room and temple are four fantastic creatures. They are patterned on the cherubim of Ezekiel's vision, which John follows fairly closely, while remodelling the details. In Ezekiel, the cherubim who support, and form the wheels of, God's chariot throne have four faces (Ezekiel 1:6, 10, 20). In Revelation those faces have become four separate creatures, which in Jewish thought represented the greatest of God's creatures. So here the four living creatures stand for all created beings.

They are full of eyes, which we have seen to be associated with God's Spirit, and so represent God's watchful awareness of his creation. The creator is intimately involved with his world. In the Bible, creation is not simply God's initial act of making, but his continued preservation and sustaining of all that exists. Together the creatures sing John's adaptation of the song of the seraphim in Isaiah's vision of God (Isaiah 6:3).

This is the purpose of creation, to give glory to God by its very existence, and to sing his praise (verse 11).

The coming one

God is described as the one 'who was', for he predates all things, and everything has its being through him. He is the one 'who is', for despite his hiddenness from sinful human sight, and despite many appearances to the contrary, God is still there to be known, served and worshipped. And God is the one who 'is to come' in final victory, bringing judgment and salvation. Perhaps there is a hint here of the mysterious longing of creation for its redemption and renewal which Paul mentions in Romans 8:19ff.

In this chapter the emphasis is on God as creator, but true to the biblical tradition, John cannot be satisfied simply with creation. There are hints throughout of God's redeeming work: the presence of the twenty-four elders, the sea of destruction and redemption. In the rest of the Bible, creation is almost always linked with the need for redemption (Genesis 1 and Psalm 8 are the exceptions).

In our time there is a renewed emphasis on the spirituality of creation, both within Christianity and various strands of 'New Age' thought. Modern-day paganism and witchcraft, and Christian creation spirituality, as well as less coherent forms of mysticism, all stress the unity of creation and of the place of human beings within it. This ties in with a proper concern for the environment and ecological awareness. Yet for there to be true hope, we need the awareness of the need for redemption both of sinful humanity and of the world in which we live. The Christian hope is for a new creation which encompasses all that God has made.

Eternal worship

So the people of God, the elders, join their voices with the song of creation, and praise their creator. In court ceremonial, they offer their crowns as kingly subjects of their high king.

This is the essence of worship. It combines both praise and self-offering to the one whose very presence is both glorious and infinitely desirable.

All worshippers have surely at some time gained the sense that their worship is joining in with the praises of heaven and all creation. Those brief flashes of exalted experience are in fact windows into the reality which John reminds us is the actual truth. Worship is the business of heaven and earth, and whether we feel it or not, our worship, from the grandest cathedral to the humblest prayer group, is a part of that perpetual praise and service.

PRAYER

Father, give us in our worship an awareness of the eternal worship of which we are a part.

22

The great reversal

Having set the scene of heaven's worship of its creator, John continues to follow the pattern of Ezekiel's vision, for he now sees a scroll in the hand of God (Ezekiel 2:9f). Like Ezekiel's scroll, it is written on the front and back, which indicates the great amount of its contents.

Scholars have argued for years as to what exactly the scroll signifies. The seven seals have been taken to indicate a legal document, such as a will. Others have seen it as the book of life containing the list of all the redeemed. Others see it as the original of the Jewish Law given to Moses, and yet others as the forecast of events to come. But the fact is that we are not told here what its contents are. All we can be sure of at this stage is that it is a book of immense importance. Eventually we shall find that it contains God's plan for the final triumph of his kingdom.

So a mighty angel calls for one who is worthy to open it. This is no ordinary book, and it will need an extraordinary person to break the seals.

Tears in heaven

No one comes forward, and John weeps at the loss. It is a moment of purely human relief in the drama of heaven. Amidst the awesome events of God's court, a human being sheds tears. It is also an affirmation that God has room in his designs for human weakness and human feelings.

Conquering lion

John is not left desolate for long. One of the elders, who act throughout the book as a kind of chorus, tells him that the Lion of Judah, the Root of David, has conquered, and can open the book.

Both of these descriptions are titles of the Messiah. In Genesis 49:9, as Jacob blesses his sons, Judah is described as a lion's whelp. So the Messiah, who was to come from the tribe of Judah, became the Lion of Judah, a term which occurs among other places in the Dead Sea scrolls (the library of a Jewish sect from Qumran, by the Dead Sea).

An even more popular messianic passage was Isaiah 11:1–10, where a new king of the house of David is foretold. He will spring up like a new shoot from the root of Jesse (Isaiah 11:2) and bring the time of peace and well-being.

Sacrificial lamb

The images of conquest and power are what John hears, but what he sees is different: a Lamb bearing the marks of sacrifice. To be sure, it is a Lamb with power, for horns are a symbol of strength. Yet the strength of this Lamb lies in its passage through death to new life.

It is, of course, Jesus. The images of conquest and power are correct, but John is telling us that the victory comes about through the self-sacrificing love which took Jesus to the cross. Real victory comes only to the one who lays down his life.

It is the prime example of the principle which runs through the teaching of Jesus: that love and forgiveness, sacrifice and service are the true values of the kingdom of God. The way of Christ turns the values of the world upside down. It is through these new values, lived out to the point of death, that Jesus is worthy to reveal the destiny of the world, for the destiny of the world is made possible through his death and resurrection.

PRAYER

Father, help us not to be seduced by the world's definitions of success, but to seek the love and service which mark those who share in the rule of heaven.

23 The Lamb enthroned

The final characteristic of the Lamb is its seven eyes, which are the seven spirits. Jesus is the giver of the Holy Spirit. In Zechariah 4:10 the seven eyes of God range throughout the world. So we are being told that the Spirit who ranges the world, and who is the motivating force of the Church, is the Spirit of Jesus. It is through the Spirit that the presence of Jesus is made real to his people.

The Spirit is therefore intimately connected both with God and with Christ, a further hint at the threefold nature of the divine which was to become the doctrine of the Trinity.

The king takes his throne

Verses 5–8 are widely recognized as being based on an eastern enthronement ceremony, in which the new king is presented along with his credentials, and then enthroned.

John's vision of the Lamb of power who is also the conquering Lion of Judah is the presentation of Christ as the king. Yet this king has conquered by self-sacrifice, through which he becomes the giver of the Spirit of life.

He approaches the throne of God and takes the scroll that only he is worthy to open. We should suppose that he also takes his place on the throne with God, for in 7:17 the Lamb is 'at the centre of the throne'.

Once he has taken his place, the heavenly court fall down before him and offer a new song. In the Old Testament, the call to 'sing a new song' to the Lord marks particular acts of deliverance and victory by God (e.g. Psalm 98:1; Isaiah 42:10). In this case the victory is the supreme triumph of the cross. John is presenting in this passage the spiritual reality which lies behind Calvary. The death of the Messiah, and his resurrection and ascension, is his enthronement over all creation.

It is significant that the elders hold censers which represent the prayers of the saints. The risen Christ is now, with God, the recipient of the prayers of the Church.

Christ our Passover

The sacrificial Lamb calls to mind the lamb of Passover, the festival of deliverance from Egyptian slavery. This connection is made clear in the song of the court. He has ransomed his people, as from slavery, and made them a kingdom and priests (cf. Exodus 19:6).

What is more, he has ransomed them from all the peoples of the earth. Here for the first time we meet the strongly universalist strain of Revelation. Salvation is not intended for one particular race or nation, but for all. The first exodus resulted in the choosing of Israel. The final exodus is open to all.

According to NRSV, the redeemed will rule on earth. However, there is a variant reading in some ancient manuscripts which has the present tense—'they reign on earth'. At first sight, this is more difficult to understand, and so is to be preferred as the correct reading (because a change from an easy meaning to a more obscure one is less likely).

If this reading is correct, it sounds a note of encouragement for a beleaguered Church. What to the world may seem weak, outmoded and powerless already has a share in the kingship of Christ. Those who suffer for their faith, who are called to witness in their poor and stumbling way to the gospel of Jesus, are already royal priests, mediating the love of their king to the world.

This is more than a word of spiritual comfort. It sets up the Church as an alternative to the power systems of the world. The Church can rule, not by the methods of the world, but by providing for its members an alternative concept of community, based on love, equality and forgiveness. To those outside that community, its presence should be a witness to the possibility of a fellowship based on love and service. The Church is called to be living proof of a different authority.

PRAYER

Lord Jesus Christ, as you have done so much for us, and so .
gained a crown, may we reflect your love and sacrifice to those
around us.

24
Crescendo

The heavenly worship builds to a crescendo as countless angels add their voices to the song of the elders and the four creatures. You may have had the experience of hearing some piece of music build to a glorious conclusion and wished that somehow that moment of triumphant exultation could last forever. Here in heaven it does. That seems to be the effect that John is aiming for.

The hymn to the Lamb is more than verbal fireworks, though. It follows closely the pattern of the hymn to God in 4:11. God is worthy because he created. The Lamb is worthy because he was slaughtered. Both hymns are based on a recognition of what the one who is worshipped has done.

It is often said that the sheer vision of God or Christ is the basis of the purest worship, and the goal of mystics, both Jewish and Christian, has been to seek the vision of God. Certainly the *trisagion* (Holy, holy, holy...) of 4:8 is the response of the heavenly court to the presence of God. Yet the longer and more substantial hymns recount the deeds of God and the Lamb. Worship is rooted as much in thankful response to God's acts as in anything else.

It is when the people of God recognize the extent of his love through his acts of creation and redemption that worship follows. This is not a lesser sort of worship, as though there were something wrongly selfish about responding to God's gift. He is not bribing us to worship. God is not a passive object of reverence but an actor in his own drama. His true character can be appreciated only in his actions, which are those of a giver. We are created to receive God's love. He is not a narcissist who needs to be admired by his fans, but an artist who pours himself into his creation and a parent who gives himself to his children. Worship is the response to such boundless giving that it pours out beyond the limitless confines of God's own being and takes shape in creation and in creation's redemption.

Giving to God

This makes sense of what at first seems a contradiction. In both 4:11 and 5:12 God and the Lamb are worthy to receive glory, honour, power, wealth and so on. (It is characteristic of John's style that he never repeats a phrase exactly, though the sense and structure remain recognizably the same.)

We may ask how God can receive more of these qualities than he already has by nature. In an absolute sense, of course, he cannot. In the language of worship, though, he can. It is in the human response to God that these attributes are recognized, and shown to be fitting for God's character. He is not only almighty and all-knowing; he has also shown himself through his acts to be worthy of such power and might. In a real sense, by offering himself as our object of worship, God stands under human judgment. The worship of his people is their discernment that he is worthy to receive such praise.

Of course, such judgment is two-edged. Those who fail to recognize the absolute fact of God's worthiness in the end judge themselves, for they have failed to recognize the eternal truth that undergirds creation.

Holy Trinity

Finally the chorus of praise spreads out beyond the limits of heaven to embrace all that exists, as every creature sings praise to God and to the Lamb.

The same praise is offered to the Lamb as to God. When we add to this the close relation of the seven spirits who are the Holy Spirit to God and to Christ, we are as close to the doctrine of the Trinity as we can get without using the word. In Revelation there are those who receive worship: God, Christ and the Spirit. There are those who worship: the elders, the four creatures, the angels and all creation (cf. 19:9f). That is to say, the holy Trinity is worshipped by all that is made.

PRAYER

Holy, holy, holy, Lord God almighty...

25

The seven seals

Revelation was definitely written so that it would yield much to careful study. At the same time we need to remember that its main audience would be those who listened to it as it was read aloud. This helps to explain its structure. John uses recurring patterns of phrases, numbers and symbols which would stick in the minds of his hearers and help them to understand his message.

One of these patterns is a set of three series of seven judgments (seven seals: 6:1—8:5; seven trumpets: 8:2—11:19; seven bowls: 15:1—16:21). These 'seven-series' are linked together and each consists of a set of four judgments followed by a set of three, suggesting disasters on earth and judgments from heaven. The first two seven-series also contain interludes showing the role of the saints in the events described.

For those who see Revelation as a detailed prophecy of events still to come, the seven-series foretell a future of increasing disaster on earth, as God lets loose his judgment prior to the final coming of Christ. This is unlikely. Each of the seven-series ends with the end of the world (6:12–17; 11:15–19; 16:17–21).

The series of judgments each tell the history of the world from different perspectives, and with different emphases. John has written several accounts which complement each other, rather than trying to fit everything into one simple narrative. So Revelation keeps going over the same ground, but each time adds a new dimension, showing new ways of interpreting the world's story, the Church's situation, and the hope of humankind.

Words of Jesus

In Mark 13, with its parallels in Matthew 24 and Luke 21, we find the source of the seven seals. There Jesus spoke of the end time, and the signs of its coming: wars, earthquakes, famine, persecution and the shaking of the heavens (Mark 13:7ff, 24ff). John probably knew, if not the actual Gospels, the story which lay behind the Gospel accounts. He drops the bits about the fall of Jerusalem (Mark

13:14–19), which in his day was already in the past. He also leaves out the warning against false prophets (Mark 13:21–23) for he will deal with that issue elsewhere.

For both Jesus and John, these are not a catalogue of signs which will one day come to pass, but a description of the way the world is, and a key to understanding world events in the light of God's coming kingdom. In that sense, we are told, the current age is the last days. Since the coming of Jesus, all the world's history has been the history of the last days. This is not because his coming is imminent in time, for no one knows the time in history of his coming (Mark 13:32f), but because all life must now be lived in the light of that coming.

Living in hope

John has adapted the words of Jesus to help his readers understand their own situation. This is the continuing task of God's people: to take the message of Jesus and apply it to their own day.

As we look at the events of our world, we are called to interpret them in the light of Christ. Wars and violence must still be met with a message of reconciliation, and a warning of judgment. Ecological disaster and exploitation calls for a reminder of humanity's responsibility to its creator. Economic exploitation demands a message of concern for the poor and powerless. Persecution calls for faithful and courageous witness. Tears in the fabric of society tell of judgment on materialism and individualism, and ask for a message of community which should be modelled by the people of God.

PRAYER

Father, enable us to take the gospel message, and speak it boldly to the world of today.

26
Violence

As the Lamb opens each of the first four seals of the scroll, one of the four living creatures who represent creation calls, 'Come!' The invitation is not to the rider, but to Christ, whose coming is signposted by the turmoil on earth.

The inspiration for the four riders is Zechariah 1:8–10 and 6:1–8 where coloured horses pull chariots which patrol the earth and bring God's judgment to the nations. Unlike those of Zechariah, the colour of John's horses is significant.

Conquest

The first horse is white, and represents conquest. Some commentators see this as the triumphant progress of the gospel, or of Christ, because of the colour and the crown. But white for John is not the colour of heaven or of the saints, but simply the sign of victory. There are earthly victories, brought about by the power of armies, but they are victories only of fear. John's readers would know of the defeat of the Roman armies by the mounted archers of Parthia in AD62. This empire, built on the ruins of Persia, remained a threat to Rome and a source of fear to the eastern empire for centuries.

The conquering hero on a white horse, the symbol of victory, looks at first sight to be a strange image of the judgment of God. Yet such conquest is achieved only by pain and suffering. The much vaunted Roman peace, the *pax Romana* which Roman propaganda held up as one of the great benefits of the empire, was based on the grim reality of the legions, and the iron grip of Roman rule.

War

The glamorous image of the conqueror is in reality based on the red of carnage. The empire was not, in John's day, much at war. Yet many would remember the 'year of four emperors', a time of civil strife which followed Nero's suicide in AD68. For Jewish Christians, the rebellion of Judea, culminating in the fall of Jerusalem in AD70 was a recent reminder of the reality of Roman peace.

Nearly two thousand years later, war is still the mainstay of human activity. The greatest conflicts of human history are a living memory, and since the Second World War, more lives have been lost to warfare than in the two world wars combined.

The Middle East, Northern Ireland, Central America, have become bywords for civil conflict. All these, says John, are the judgment of God and the herald of the new age.

Judgment of the nations

Are we seriously to say that God sends wars to punish humanity? It seems far from the actions of a loving God. Such a question misses the point.

Firstly, it is not so much that God sends them, as that they are the natural consequences of human sin. God's judgment lies in his acceptance of those consequences. In Romans Paul wrote that God had 'given up' sinful humanity to the consequences of sin (Romans 1:24, 26, 28). The judgment of God consists in having to lie in the bed we have made.

Secondly, though, there is hope. The consequences of estrangement from God are grim—a world given over to greed, self-interest and strife. Yet those very consequences may just make us look for some other way, a way which lies open to the eye of faith, and is found in Jesus Christ. That hope is not great, if all that we see is the judgment itself; a point John sees clearly (9:20). But as we shall see, judgment goes hand in hand with the call to repentance

PRAYER

Lord help us to hear above the turmoil of war, your call to peace.

Famine and death

War brings with it other horrors, famine and disease. The shortage signified by the third rider is survivable, but harsh. The staple diet of grain sells at over ten times its proper price. The slightly more luxurious commodities of oil and wine are still available though. For those with money, life goes on, but the poor, as always, can barely survive.

Hidden amidst the picture of the judgment of God is another judgment—the call for justice. Just as the harshest words for the churches were reserved for the wealthy, so here John betrays his sympathy for the poor.

It is a sympathy which the Bible ascribes to God as well. Part of the condemnation of the sinful world is that in times of shortage the poor suffer as much as they do. Part of the message of Revelation is the call for justice in the world.

Pale horse coming

The Greek word translated as 'pale' literally means green, here the colour of a corpse. There is a word-play which is hidden from us, for in Greek 'death' can also mean pestilence, in the wake of which comes Hades, the lord of the dead, gathering the victims of battlefield, famine and disease.

The reference to death by wild animals conjures up the terrible fate of some of the wounded in war. It also forms a link with the next seal, and the vision of Christian martyrs, some of whom would have met their end in the arena, as fuel for the insatiable blood-lust of the Roman mob.

For all its horror, this vision, and that of the preceding three riders, brings only a limited judgment (a quarter of the earth is affected). It presages the final judgment, but does not yet bring it. This gives us another indication that we are looking at a picture of the present state of the world, seen as the end times (as are all times since the resurrection). At this stage, judgment is still limited, for there is yet time for repentance, if only these events are seen for what they are—God's warning shot across the bows of the world.

Delight in death?

Blood-lust is a charge which is often enough levelled against the Book of Revelation itself. We have seen that John interprets the strife of the world as God's judgment and call to repentance. Does he also delight in the same vision as the crowd in the amphitheatre, though reserving that fate for enemies of the Church?

I think not. He presents the terrible fate of so many of the world's inhabitants as a call to see that fate as less terrible than it could be. For Christians, death is not the worst that can happen. It is instead the gateway to eternal life, and is far less dreadful than denial of their Lord. The very fact that death is seen as the ultimate fate is a sign of the lack of hope in a world without God.

The real question he poses is, where do we turn for hope in the face of invasion and civil war, famine, disease and persecution? In an age of terrorism, AIDS, global warming and international injustice, where is there hope for the world?

The immediate passage does not answer the question, which is asked directly at verse 17, but to ask the question is to prepare the way of the answer. Or rather, we should say, the Answer, for he is coming; and the turmoil of the world prepares his way, and calls us to be ready for him.

PRAYER

Lord, may your coming find us prepared, by our witness to you, to your justice and your compassion.

28
Call for justice

The opening of the fifth seal introduces another aspect of judgment. John sees the souls of the martyrs under the altar. This is the altar in God's heavenly throne-room temple, on which both incense and blood sacrifices are offered (the Jerusalem temple had separate altars). In the earthly temple the blood of sacrifices was poured out at the base of the altar. Here the lives of those witnesses (the meaning of the Greek word, martyr) are presented as sacrifices offered to God.

The idea of martyrs as sacrifices was common in Jewish thought, where their death was seen as an atonement for the sins of Israel (4 Maccabees 17:22). For Christians atonement is the work of Christ alone, but the image of sacrifice is still applied (cf. Philippians 2:7; 2 Timothy 4:6; Letter of Ignatius to the Romans 2:2). The faithful witness of those who have died for their faith is the ultimate act of self-offering to God. So John sees those who have made the supreme sacrifice kept safely under the watchful care of God.

This is part of the answer to the objection that Revelation is full of death. It is not. It is full of the promise of eternal life, which is held up as the alternative to death for all who have faith.

How long?

The martyred souls cry out for vengeance, which is a far cry from Jesus' own call for forgiveness. Or so it may seem. In the Bible, though, abstract ideas are often clothed in personal language. God's reply suggests that the real thought is of vindication. How long will it be before the inhabitants of the earth are seen to be wrong, and the witness of the saints justified?

From the world's perspective, the death of martyrs is their defeat. It takes the eye of faith to see the reality—that they are clothed in the white of victory. In the end, the judgment of the world will be reversed by the judgment of God, and the cause of the martyrs will be shown to be right.

Until then, they must wait, for they have a role in God's plan. It is a common theme in apocalyptic writing that the vindication of the martyrs must wait until God's purposes are fulfilled (cf. 1 Enoch 47). At the moment, the role of the martyrs is still unclear, though all will be explained (11:3–13). Until then, it is enough to know that martyrdom will continue, and that God sees it as necessary.

Justice for the innocent

A second meaning of the martyrs' call is a demand for justice. Not only must they be seen to have been right, but justice must be done. They have been falsely condemned, and the cause of justice has been betrayed. Like the blood of Abel (Genesis 4:10), the shed blood of the innocent calls for a reckoning.

In that sense the martyrs stand not only for God's cause, but for all who are falsely accused and put to death. Today as much as at any time, the innocent suffer for the sake of expediency and ideology. Whether it is the silenced voices of political dissent, or the eliminated street children, or the conveniently ignored deaths of farmers who stand in the way of 'development', blood still cries for justice.

Part of the witness of the people of God is a witness to his justice. The followers of one who was himself the innocent victim of political cynicism are surely called to be witnesses to justice in this world; to be themselves a foretaste of the coming justice of God.

PRAYER

Father, open the eyes of your people to the injustice of the world, and their mouths to proclaim your judgment.

Standing before God

The opening of each seal on the scroll of God is accompanied by a vision of God's judgment. None of these is the content of the scroll, for until all have been opened, the scroll itself cannot be read. They are preparations for the reading of the scroll, which will put in motion the events it contains.

Now we approach the climax of the breaking of the seals. The end of creation as we know it has arrived. All that remains is the final judgment. In a great cataclysm, all that seems most stable, stars, mountains and islands, are shifted out of place. This is language borrowed from the standard apocalyptic vocabulary of the day, drawing on the imagery of the Old Testament (Isaiah 13:9ff; 2:10ff; 34:4; Ezekiel 32:7f; 38:19; Hosea 10:8; Joel 2:10, 30f; Amos 8:8). None of it is a literal description of what one day will actually happen, and those who try to see a prediction of nuclear war, cosmic catastrophe or whatever have missed the point.

When all that seems most steadfast in the world is stripped away, there is nothing to come between human beings and the vision of God. Then they must face him, and the consequences of their deeds. Here the result is fear and mourning. The vision of God does not provoke worship, but only a desire to hide.

Love and wrath

This is perhaps the best image of the judgment of God. It is not the image of a law court, where God tries the case of each, and pronounces salvation or damnation. It is the response of those who have held God at a distance throughout their lives and find that is no longer possible. In their lives they have fostered an attitude and an approach to life which carries with it nothing of the world to come; and so there is nothing left which is compatible with the vision of God. The response to God during this world's history has been negative, and it is the only response which is now left. In the end we must respond to God, perceiving either his love or his wrath.

As the awful result of sin is revealed, people of every station in life find themselves in the same situation. Wealth and power are ultimately no shield, and all ask the same question: 'Who is able to stand' in the face of God and his Messiah? The judgment falls on everyone, but the powerful and the rich are mentioned in particular, since they are the prime movers in the sinful structures of a world which tries to exist without God. This point will be come clearer as John's message unfolds.

It is a bleak vision, but is it the only one? We noted that the response of people to the coming of Christ in 1:7 could be taken in two ways, as despair or repentance. Does the present passage leave only the possibility of despair? As things stand, yes it does. But this is only one perspective on the world's history and the coming of the kingdom of God. Human sinfulness has resulted in injustice, the destruction of peoples' lives and the death of the saints of God. The culmination of such a path is irrevocable destruction. There are, though, other perspectives, and these too need to be explored.

For the present we can note that 21:24 envisages the kings of the earth, who now cower before the coming God, entering the city of God with tributes of worship. How these two possibilities can be held together will unfold as John shares his vision with us.

PRAYER

Heavenly Father, the time will come when we meet you face to face, and see in Christ the vision of your love. Give us grace to live our lives by faith in you, so that our final vision will be one of infinite joy.

30

Belonging to God

Before the final seal is opened comes an interlude in which the powers of destruction are held back till the servants of God are marked with the seal of God. Once again, John borrows his image from Ezekiel, where executioners pass through Jerusalem, slaying all who have not been marked on the forehead with the sign of loyalty to God (Ezekiel 9:4–6).

To call the present passage an interlude, though, is slightly misleading. Chapter 7 is part of a series of visions which runs parallel to the visions of judgment. Chapters 4 and 5 showed the heavenly reality which lies behind the events of earthly history, and in which the events on earth are rooted. Chapter 7 now looks at the status of the people of God amidst the judgments on earth. In the second seven-series, beginning at 8:2, 6 comes the third alternative vision, in which the people of God are seen to be the bringers of hope to those who suffer God's judgment. So there is a sequence of judgment which alternates with a sequence of salvation.

Chapter 7 also ties together the seals and the trumpets which follow. Connecting with the seals-series, it answers the despairing question of those who cannot hide from the wrath of the Lamb: 'Who is able to stand?' (6:17). Those who are marked with the seal of God, and who are before his throne (7:9), are able to stand.

Property of God

The image of the seal suggests ownership—the servants of God bear his stamp (more literally, his slaves are branded!), and are marked as belonging to him. So they will be brought safely through the great ordeal (7:14) which marks the coming of God's victory. This does not mean that they will be protected from physical harm. Both experience and the words of Jesus suggest otherwise (Mark 13:9–13). Christians are a part of the world, and are not immune from the disasters brought by the four riders of 6:1–8. What they do have is hope, and the ability to see these as part of God's activity and opportunities for his service. Where the world sees only destruction and

74

hardship, the Church is told to proclaim repentance and trust in God.

The seal is a protection from the spiritual dangers which follow in the wake of the warning judgments of God. This is where the interlude connects with the coming seven trumpets. The winds which are held back by the four angels suggest a new spate of judgments, and in fact tie in well with the ecological disasters of 8:6–12 rather than the human violence of the first four seals.

The vision of the seven seals has dealt only with physical hardships, but as the seven trumpets will make clear, these carry spiritual consequences. There is the possibility that they will bring about repentance, an awareness of human limitations and the need for meaning and hope from beyond the confines of human life. But they may lead to the rejection of God, and the placing of hope in that which is other than the almighty creator.

Faced with human mortality, we search not for the hope of eternal life, but for ways of extending human life for a few more years, at whatever cost. Faced with events beyond our control, we are tempted to seek means of controlling the world through our own strength, or we turn to superstitions, seeking out clairvoyants, astrologers and other false sources of comfort.

Those sealed with the seal of God have a hope which looks beyond the confines of this life, and in so doing, enriches the present life. Moreover, it is no shame to admit that life is often beyond our control. What is terrible, is to have no faith in the God who is himself in control.

PRAYER

Father, when I am tempted to forget you or to place my trust in that which is less than you, remind me that I belong to you, and that you hold me safe.

31 Ready for battle

It is tempting to wonder whether the sealing of God's servants is purely John's symbolism. In the New Testament, 'seal' is used to describe God's gift of the Holy Spirit (Ephesians 1:13; 4:30) and is Paul's description of circumcision (Romans 4:11), to which baptism corresponds. Since the gift of the Spirit and baptism are closely linked (e.g. 1 Corinthians 12:13) it may well be that John intends a reminder of the permanent nature of baptism, both as a sign of God's steadfastness and a call to his service.

The call to service is certainly in view in these verses, where John hears the number of the sealed as 144,000, drawn from the twelve tribes of Israel. In fact, the list of tribes is rather strange. Judah comes first, rather than Reuben, the first-born son of Jacob, because the Messiah is of the tribe of Judah. But Dan is not mentioned, and is replaced by Manasseh, one of the sons of Joseph. This may be because Dan was seen as the rebellious tribe (Genesis 49:17), but it is just as likely that the list was inaccurately rattled off from memory, since the actual tribes were only of historic interest, and do not matter to John.

The people of God

What does matter is the symbolism. 144,000 is the square of the number of the tribes of Israel, multiplied by 1,000. Once we realize that the number is symbolic, many interpretations of the list of those sealed cease to carry much weight. John is not speaking of literal Jews, as for instance, a remnant of faithful Israel. Neither is he speaking of a select number of Christians, such as the martyrs, or, as the Jehovah's Witnesses would have us believe, a specially blessed band of the redeemed. In fact, those sealed must represent all Christians, or we would be left with the strange notion that some believers are sealed by God to protect them from the time of trial, while others are not. And if we are right in seeing an allusion to baptism, then those sealed are certainly all the faithful.

This becomes clear in verse 9 where John sees a great multitude before the throne of God. He is using the same contrast between what is heard and what is seen, as we met at 5:5–6. There he heard of the triumph of the Lion of Judah, but saw a Lamb. Yet the Lion and the Lamb were the same. Here he hears of the sealing of 144,000, but sees a numberless host, which turns out to be in fact the same people. Those sealed are all Christians, described in terms of Israel, for the followers of Jesus now stand as the people of God (Romans 9:6–8).

The army of the Lord

Why then does John speak of the people of God as a selection from the tribes of Israel? The clue is found in the Old Testament, where a census of tribes, and a levy from them, is sanctioned by God only for times of war, when men over the age of twenty are counted. The likely model for John's picture is the census of Numbers 1. The people of God are characterized as God's army, called to his service to fight for his holy cause.

There is an interesting parallel here with one of the Dead Sea scrolls, known as the War Scroll, which describes the coming final conflict between the 'sons of light' and the 'sons of darkness', the pagan nations. This is expected to be a literal war, and the members of the Qumran community are given detailed explanations of troop placements, tactics and the way the war is expected to go.

John's image of the final war is different. Just as he transformed the Jewish nationalism of the Lion of Judah into the universal sacrifice of the Lamb that was slaughtered, so he transforms the final conflict from one of literal warfare to one of sacrificial witness.

PRAYER

Father, as you call us to be yours, so keep us as your faithful soldiers and servants.

32 The company of heaven

After *hearing* the number of those sealed, John *sees* a great multitude which seems to contrast in every way with the 144,000. Whereas the number sealed referred to the church on earth (verses 1–3), the multitude stands before the throne of God in heaven. Unlike the carefully counted army of the Lord, those in heaven are uncountable. The numbered saints are depicted as drawn from the tribes of Israel, whereas the multitude is from every nation, tribe, people and language. None the less, they are the same people of God.

The 144,000 are the Church on earth, called to fight for God against those who oppose him. That is the present significance of God's people: his servants who carry out his mission in the world of conflict between God and evil. The present vision takes us forward to the final destiny of the followers of Jesus. They have endured the great ordeal which is the current experience of the Church, and which prefigures the final victory of God (verse 14). Now they join in the eternal hymn of praise to God, becoming in reality what is presently symbolized by the twenty-four elders—part of the worshipping company of heaven. In the language of later theology, the 144,000 represent the 'Church militant' and the multitude stand for the 'church triumphant'.

The palm branches they hold are reminiscent of the Jewish Feast of Tabernacles, the most joyful of the annual festivals. Tabernacles combined harvest thanksgiving and thanks for God's gift of the land with celebration of the rededication of the temple by the Maccabees. So these are those who have entered into the heavenly promised land, as the harvest of God's salvation, and who now worship in the heavenly temple.

Their song praises God for the salvation he has achieved, and praises the Lamb through whom he has brought about that salvation. It provides heaven's reply to the cry of 'Hosanna' ('save us') on the lips of those who waved palm branches at Jesus' entry into Jerusalem (John 12:13). The presence of the multitude in heaven calls forth further worship from the heavenly court, for this is the final proof of God's victory, and the victory of his people. They have gained the promises held out in the seven messages to the churches to 'everyone who conquers'. In them, drawn from all the peoples of the earth to be God's own people, the promise to the patriarchs of Israel that their descendants would be innumerable (Genesis 13:16) has been fulfilled.

Family of God

It is one of the great tragedies of the Church's history that Christians have failed to live up to this vision. Those who have, by God's grace, been grafted onto the stock of his chosen people (Romans 11:17ff) and included in the promises to Abraham (Galatians 3:29), have been the greatest persecutors of God's people, the Jews. Those who are destined to be a countless multitude drawn from all races and nationalities have fostered nationalism and racism, and continue to do so.

Catholic and Protestant in Northern Ireland, Orthodox and Catholic in Serbia and Bosnia, have taken Christian tags and used them to identify warring parties. The terrible tribal genocide in Rwanda in 1994 saw Christians divided by tribe rather than united by a common faith. 'Tribal blood is thicker than the water of baptism,' said one bishop.

At the same time, the vision provides hope to many. Those who are tempted to see themselves as part of a small, struggling congregation, or a faith that in much of the Western world seems to have been left behind by secular societies, may look again at John's vision and see the reality behind the illusion of the present moment.

In those very places which are examples of Christian failure, Church communities still struggle to bring about reconciliation and healing. Salvation, which means wholeness, health and well-being, and in Hebrew means also victory, belong to our God; and to those who see the vision, and in it conquer.

PRAYER

Father, give to your divided and warring people a renewed vision of the diversity and unity of the company of heaven.

Strange conquest

The people of God have conquered, but how? They have fought as God's army, but John surely does not imagine a literal battle. In fact John is using the same contrast as at 5:5–6. Just as the victory of the Lion of Judah turns out to be the death of the Lamb of God, so the victory of God's army is the death of his martyrs.

This multitude, explains one of the elders, is those who have come out of the great ordeal, washing their robes in the blood of the Lamb. Although this is usually taken as a reference to Christ's sacrifice which cleanses believers from sin, it is more likely to be a reference to the effect of the believers' own martyrdom. The shedding of their blood in faithful witness to Christ joins them with his death. It allows them to share in his sacrifice, and hence in his victory.

This may seem a strange idea to readers brought up on the doctrine of the total sufficiency of the death of Christ. However, the death of the martyrs has no saving power in itself—it draws its significance from the death and victory of the Lamb. In a similar way, Paul saw his suffering as sharing, indeed completing, the sufferings of Jesus (Colossians 1:24). It becomes clear that John is referring to martyrdom when we look at 12:11, where the saints defeat Satan 'by the blood of the Lamb and by the word of their testimony, for they did not cling to life even in the face of death'. Here John uses the Hebrew poetic technique of parallel statements which express the same idea in different and complementary ways—a style we are familiar with from the Psalms. So in 12:11 the 'word of their testimony' even to the point of death qualifies and explains 'the blood of the Lamb'.

The white robes, then, are the victory garments of those who have conquered by dying as faithful witnesses to Jesus. In this way, John turns the imagery of holy war on its head. True victory is not found in earthly conquest, or Hollywood heroics, but in steadfast refusal to compromise with the enemies of God, even to the point of death. Those who are marked with the seal of God, and numbered as his army, are marked out for martyrdom.

If this seems a strange way of ensuring the safety of God's people, we need to remember that the sealing of the servants of God is not to protect them from physical danger. It is to protect them from spiritual peril, from bowing down to the forces of persecution and oppression, and so losing their faith in God. After all, the victory of Christ comes through the cross. Should his followers expect less (John 15:18–20)?

Loyal witnesses

If those sealed, and the great crowd in heaven, are the whole people of God, and are the martyrs, does this mean that John expects the whole Church to suffer death for its faith? Or does he count as true Christians only those who die for their faith? The answer is neither. In the symbolic world of Revelation, the Church is defined as those who die for Christ. But in reality, he knows that not all will do so, either in his own time, or (probably) in the distant future. Yet if all Christians were wiped out in some great persecution, this would not be a defeat, but the final victory. It would be a victory for the martyrs who pass in the final exodus to heaven, and we will find later, it would be a victory for God's plan of salvation.

At this stage of his book John is making two points. In the persecution he sees looming over his own churches, and in the life of the church at large, Christians are called to be faithful witnesses to Jesus, no matter what may come; and if the worst comes (in earthly terms) it is no less than the triumphant completion of salvation.

John's picture is deliberately exaggerated, but it is worth pondering the often quoted statistic that the twentieth century has seen more Christian martyrs than all the rest of the Church's history.

PRAYER

Father, thank you for the example of the many who have remained faithful to you in the face of death. Deepen our trust and strengthen our witness.

34 Return of the exiles

The multitude of the redeemed stand before the throne of God because they have shared in the sacrifice of Christ. This does not mean that their witness and martyrdom have earned them a place in heaven. Their place is the gift of God through Christ's death. They have reached the promised goal because they have clung to faith, and not given in to the temptation to deny Christ, and with him their salvation.

John does not teach a salvation by works. What he does insist on, is the responsibility which is the consequence of salvation. God's grace is free, but it comes as a call to service and in Revelation that service is to bear witness to Jesus.

Service continues in heaven. The word translated by NRSV as 'worship' can also mean service, with the connotation of carrying out religious duties. There is work to be done even in heaven; the joyful work of worship.

Promise

In this vision John is allowed to look ahead to the final day of victory. The references to the water of life and God's wiping away of tears look ahead to 21:4 and 22:1. The triumph of the heavenly Church will come, but it is not yet here, and in the middle of verse 15 the tense changes from the present of immediate vision to the future of promised blessing. The time will come when God will stretch his tent over them (the more literal meaning of 'shelter'), but for now worship is a faint foretaste of the worship of heaven, and the witness of the saints is carried out in the midst of an often hostile world.

The mention of the tent, or tabernacle, continues the Tabernacles theme of the heavenly worship, and evokes memories of the guiding presence of God in the wilderness (Exodus 13:21) and of the *shekinah*, the cloud of God's glory which dwelt in the tent of God (Exodus 40:34–38). It is also related to the word used in John 1:14 to describe the dwelling of God incarnate amongst his people.

Strangers in the world

Verses 16–17 are based on Isaiah 49:10. There the prophet offers hope to the Israelites in exile in Babylon. God will lead his people home to their own land, and along the way 'they shall not hunger or thirst, neither scorching wind nor sun shall strike them down, for he who has pity on them will lead them, and by springs of water will guide them.'

In this world, then, Christians are exiles, whose true homeland is in heaven, and who hold their first loyalty to the kingdom of God. This is a common theme in the New Testament. For Paul, the Christian's home city is heaven (Philippians 3:20), while in John's Gospel Jesus tells his disciples that they are not entirely part of the world in which they live (John 15:19); and Peter addresses his Christian readers as exiles of the 'Dispersion', a term used for Jews dwelling outside of the Promised Land (1 Peter 1:1).

None of this is to suggest that Christians do not play a full part in the life of God's creation, and of the societies in which they live. It does say that they must be critical of the world, and live by the values which characterize the coming kingdom. The role of the Church is to bear witness to God, and one of the ways it should do so is by holding the world up to the judgment of the kingdom of God.

From the world's point of view, the values of the kingdom are topsy-turvey. It is a kingdom in which love triumphs by self-sacrifice, in which the weak are valued and leadership is reckoned by service. It is a strange world in which a Lamb can be the shepherd.

PRAYER

Father, help us not to see the world as it sees itself, but as you see it—far from you, but deeply loved.

35 Prayer and fire

After the sealing of the saints, and the vision of their final destiny, John returns us to the opening of the seals on the scroll of God. At first sight, the opening of the seventh seal is an anti-climax. All that happens is silence.

This is because John has overlapped the end of the seal visions with the beginning of the next seven-series, the judgments introduced by seven trumpets. In this way, he shows the intimate connection between the visions of judgment. These are not three different sequences which follow on each other, but different ways of looking at the same thing. By introducing the trumpets before the seals end, he includes the trumpets within the seals. You might say that the seven-series fit within each other like Russian dolls.

A better image would be that of a microscope. As John increases the magnification, he sees that within the seventh seal there is more detail to be revealed: the seven trumpets. And they in turn will focus down into the seven bowls (15:1—16:21).

So as silence falls in heaven with the opening of the last seal, John sees the seven angels who will sound the call for the next series of judgments. These are the seven angels who, in popular Jewish thought, stood ready by God's throne as his special messengers (e.g. Tobit 12:7).

Silence in heaven

The meaning of the silence has caused much debate, but it becomes clearer when we realize that the introduction of the seven angels is best thought of as being in brackets. Then verses 3–5 follow straight on from verse 1. There was a tradition in Jewish writing that the praises of the angels in heaven stopped from time to time to allow the prayers of earth to be heard. Now, in the silence, an angel presents the prayers of the saints to God as an offering of incense on the heavenly altar.

Prayer is not unnoticed by God. It goes straight to the heart of heaven, and all the activity of heaven ceases to make way for it. It is a powerful image of the meaning and effectiveness of prayer. Prayer is the means by which the relationship of God and his people is cemented. It is the conversation of the people of God with their divine lover, and like any lover, he stops what he is doing to listen to it.

Answers on earth

Prayer does not go unanswered. The incense vessel which brought the prayers to God is now filled with the fire of heaven and sent crashing down to earth. The prayers of the saints for justice and vindication are answered by God's fire of judgment. The End, which was tottering on the brink at the opening of the sixth seal, now comes in thunder, lightning and earthquake.

These are the traditional trappings of the appearance of God, as at Mount Sinai (Exodus 19:16, 18). God comes in judgment to answer the prayers of his people.

The Bible is consistently clear that God acts in response to prayer. Not always, to be sure, in the way that those who pray might wish, but always as a response to the pleas of the faithful.

The deepest truth about prayer is that it aligns the one who prays with the will of God—that it is about learning his will, and not imposing ours. So the end result of a life of prayer is to make us want what God wants. But at the same time, we should give weight to the clear biblical theme of God's response to prayer—that prayer causes things to happen that otherwise would not. This is not to say that prayer is a magic which forces God's hand, but to affirm that he takes account of the prayers of the faithful in the way he acts in the world. Prayer acts both on the pray-er and by evoking an answer from God.

PRAYER

Lord, give me the desire to pray, and the faith to know you hear.

36

REVELATION 8:6-12
The earth recoils

Now the trumpets sound and the judgments begin (cf. Matthew 24:31). The first four seals corresponded closely to Jesus' words in Mark 13:7–8, and now the first four trumpets remind us of Mark 13:19–20, 24–25. John has used these same images and modelled them on the plagues of Egypt from Exodus 7–11. Like the Egyptian plagues they aim to make the people of the earth acknowledge God, and signal the deliverance of God's people.

As with the seal judgments, the disasters heralded by the trumpets are limited in their scope, but more intense than those of the seals. Generally, they affect a third of the earth, rather than a quarter. John is building a picture of gradually increasing suffering, which none the less allows time for a change of heart in those who are afflicted. We should not think in terms of a historical sequence of increasingly severe judgments, but of an artistic progression. The intensifying of the plagues is John's way of saying that God will do what is necessary in order to bring about repentance.

It is certainly a fact of Christian experience that human self-sufficiency needs to be set aside, often painfully, before people will acknowledge God. When they do, they find, like Paul (2 Corinthians 1:8–10) that God is the one who can see them through.

Eco-shock

Whereas the first four seal judgments were the result of human violence and injustice, the first four trumpets bring about disasters in the natural world. These in turn are, of course, God's response to human sin.

These are also appropriate to our own age. If we can see the four horsemen abroad in our own time, so we can see the effects of human sinfulness on the environment. Poor land use has devastated the centre of Russia, drying up the Caspian Sea, and changing weather patterns over north and central Asia. Deforestation brings regular disastrous flooding to Bangladesh. The Sahara desert continues to move south, swallowing once fertile lands into a sea of sand.

Pollution has destroyed large portions of the protective ozone layer, and the incidence of skin cancer increases. Weather patterns over Europe continue to change, so that it seems likely that once temperate regions will become hotter and drier, playing havoc with agriculture and destroying much of the famous English countryside.

None of this, of course, is specifically prophesied by Revelation. John knows nothing of the greenhouse effect and CFCs. But the principle of God's judgment holds firm. Those who fail to recognize the creator make free with creation in ways that it cannot sustain. The result is disastrous.

Supernatural plagues

The message of the plagues is that those who worship something other than God, be it false gods or human self-reliance, must live with the consequences. Once again, God gives up those who reject him to the results of that rejection.

The plagues here are seen as having supernatural sources (the star, Wormwood, prefigures the fall of Satan in 12:7ff—demonic evil is loose in the world). This is John's way of saying that human actions which may seem merely physical have spiritual significance. Ambitious irrigation plans may seem devoid of religious significance, but the attitude which assumes a human right to tamper with a little understood creation is spiritual pride of an immense degree. The supernatural origin of the plagues also continues to stress the element of divine judgment in what to human eyes may seem mere physical misfortune.

PRAYER

Father, give us wisdom to use properly the resources you have given us, and to recognize our responsibility to you for the world you have made, and of which we are a part.

37
Swarm of torment

The final three trumpets are heralded by an eagle, or perhaps better, a vulture. Flying high in the sky as a portent of doom (cf. Luke 17:37; Matthew 24:28), it announces the three final woes which bring human history to a close.

The first woe, at the sounding of the fifth trumpet, is a plague of locusts, but they are no ordinary insects. Echoing 8:10 a star, an angelic power, falls to earth and is allowed to open the bottomless pit. Like Wormwood, the star is an aspect of Satan's power, come to set destruction loose in the world. The fact that the key to the pit has been given to him (that is, by God) is in fact a sign of hope. For all that evil may seem irresistible, it is allowed by God as part of his plan of redemption.

The 'bottomless pit' translates the Greek term, abyss, the deep place under the earth which joins with the waters of the sea. It is the same word as the Greek version of the Old Testament uses for the formless void out of which God brought creation (Genesis 1:2). As such it symbolizes chaos and lawlessness, and is the earthly counterpart of the crystal sea of heaven. It is out of this reservoir of disorder and meaninglessness that the locusts come.

John borrows this image from Joel 2 which likens a locust swarm to God's army of judgment. Behind both Joel and John stands the locust plague of Exodus 10. Once again, the plague is intended to turn rebellious hearts to repentance.

The returns of wrong

The description of the locusts is probably borrowed from popular tradition, and is intended to heighten the sense of horror. These locusts are demonic, and attack humans, while sparing the plants. We should not see any great conflict between the death of the grass in 8:7 and its sparing from the locust horde—this is the language of symbolism, not literal description.

The plague of hellish insects brings pain, but not death, though its victims would rather die. That is, they would rather flee from God into death itself than repent and be saved.

For the locusts only harm those who are not marked with the seal of God. This is the key to understanding a vision of horror which would suit any late night film show. The seal of God does not protect his people from physical harm, but from spiritual damage. Evil is torturing only those who already worship it.

It is the very nature of evil to recoil upon its perpetrators. Those who destroy the lives and hopes of others destroy their own humanity with it. Those who deny the life of the spirit become immune to spirituality and cannot see the hope that God holds out to them. Those who claim that only the material exists or matters live out their material lives with hope of nothing greater or better.

On this level, the abyss is the cumulative power of human evil, in which all to some extent participate, and by which all are to some degree harmed. No sin is committed in a vacuum, and each wrong has its consequences both for humanity as a whole, and for sinners themselves.

Lord of destruction

Finally, John reminds us that no one is truly a free agent. We serve either God or the devil. Thus the locusts of evil have a king, unlike natural locusts (Proverbs 30:27) and it is destruction, for evil in the last analysis makes nothing, but only destroys what is good. Abaddon, the Hebrew for destruction, and Apollyon, the Greek for destroyer, are fitting titles for evil. Apollyon may also be a mockery of the Greek god Apollo, and with him emperors such as Nero and Domitian who aped the attributes of the god.

PRAYER

Father, make us aware of the consequences of our sins, and above all of the forgiveness and freedom which are found in you.

38

The wages of sin

The sixth trumpet releases the second woe: a demonic army of uncountable size. John hears the number, but could hardly carry out a head count! No earthly power could muster the number of troops John records. This is an unstoppable force, rolling over all opposition. The surprising thing is that the army kills only a third of the population.

The locust plague has probably inspired this vision, for in the Greek version of Amos 7:1 (though not the Hebrew), a locust horde is said to be commanded by the mythical Gog of Ezekiel 38:1-3. The army is led by four avenging angels from across the Euphrates, the eastern border of the Roman empire, and the boundary of the land promised to Abram (Genesis 15:18), though never in fact occupied by Israel.

None the less, although John plays on Old Testament memories of invasion (Assyria and Babylon lay beyond the Euphrates) and on Roman paranoia about Parthia, this is no human army. Death is dealt not by the riders with their colourful breastplates, but by their monstrous steeds, which in fact resemble horses only in that they are ridden.

The appointed time

It was a common motif of apocalyptic that God had an appointed time for every event. This plague comes at the precise time ordained by God, for all things are under his control.

To us this seems a disquieting idea. Is everything truly fixed? Does the history of the world, and the eternal fate of its inhabitants really run along the undeviating tram-lines of predestination? And if so, what is the point of the call to repentance?

John at this point seems to share the predetermined scheme of most apocalyptic. However, as his book unfolds, we shall see that things are not quite as cut and dried as they may appear. For now, the insistence on God's appointed hour is meant as consolation. Sin may seem supreme, the persecutors may appear in control.

But the true Lord of human history is God, and he will not be gainsaid.

Answered prayer

Like the judgment of the seventh seal, this woe comes in answer to prayer. A voice speaks from the horned altar, that is, the altar of incense. Incense so far has represented the prayers of the saints, so perhaps the voice belongs to the angel with the censer (8:3). In any case, the incense altar lets us know that prayer has been offered. Presumably this is once again the prayer for vindication of God's people. Those who have suffered persecution and rejection are shown to be right by the coming of God's judgment on the world.

The people of God are spared from the effects of this judgment, for verse 20 shows that 'humankind' here means those who are opposed to God. Once again the sparing of the saints is not a promise of freedom from earthly pain for the Church. Like the locusts, the 200 million cavalry represent the effects of sin run rampant rather than a literal military force. Interpreters who try to see in the fire, sulphur and smoke a prophecy of twentieth-century weaponry have missed the point. Fire-breathing monsters were common in mythology (see the description of Leviathan in Job 41:19–20). Here they represent the ultimate result of sin.

Sin repaid

We have seen that sin leads to destruction. The locusts represent the suffering to which wrong-doing leads. The demonic army is the final statement. Sin leads to death. To reject God is to reject the source of all life and hope, and in their absence there is nothing.

PRAYER

Father, when we are tempted, remind us of the ultimate emptiness of life without you, and the pointlessness of any apparent pleasure which interrupts the joy of knowing you.

39 The failure of judgment

At last the point of the horrors that John has unfolded in the opening of the seals and the sounding of the trumpets becomes explicit. They are intended to bring repentance. The fact that final judgment is preceded by a series of limited judgments has pointed to this conclusion, but here it is finally stated.

The judgments have been a call to turn away from the worship of that which is not God, and to give him the honour which is his alone. The primary sin is the worship of demons and idols. This is not to say that the gods represented by idols have any real existence, as Paul and the Christians of Corinth agreed (1 Corinthians 8:4-6; 10:19). However, when worship is offered to that which is not God, be it a non-existent deity or some material possession, or human ambition, or political or philosophical ideology, then demons are worshipped.

The demonic comes into being when spirituality is misdirected. Human beings are made for a commitment to God, and when their primary commitment is to something else, then it is opposed to God. That is, it is demonic.

In this sense, idolatry is the original sin and the basis of all others. When Adam and Eve listened to the serpent (Genesis 3) they gave obedience to that which was not God; they committed idolatry. When they sought to be like God through the power of knowledge (Genesis 3:5-6) they worshipped human achievement alone, and committed idolatry.

Catalogue of wrong

It is this exaltation of human desire and achievement above all else which lies behind the other sins mentioned by John. Murder and sorcery are both attempts to enforce human will on others, by control of God's creation without reference to him, and by removing human obstacles to personal power and gain. Fornication and theft are both about getting without paying—in personal commitment and love, and in fair trade.

Shocking conclusion

So with the seventh trumpet about to sound, and the total condemnation of sinful humanity waiting in the wings, do people think again—repent? No.

With a realistic assessment of human nature, John declares that those who survive carry on doing the very things which are destroying them. Like an alcoholic in search of a bottle, like a smoker ignoring the health warning, sin goes on and reaps its reward.

Or to put it another way, God has failed.

The series of judgments were meant to bring repentance. They have not. The simple fact is that whatever woes befall the world, they do not seem to result in a great turning of people to God. In fact, the victims are more likely to curse God, to blame him for 'not doing something' (exactly what he is meant to do is never specified). The suggestion that perhaps it would be good to refrain from doing the things which bring about disaster is dismissed.

Part of the reason for this is that sin is not just the action of individuals. It is tied up in the systems of the world. Much of the disastrous evil that besets humanity has no individual cause. Who is responsible for a war? Which sinner is it that is responsible for cutting down rain forests? Both are the result of economic and political forces which are beyond the control of individuals. Both are demonic; they belong to a realm of wrong which controls people rather than being controlled by human beings.

Repentance then, does not come. All that is left is for God to acknowledge that there is no hope for humanity as a whole, and to ring down the curtain. But he does not, for with God there is always hope, unimaginable as it may be.

PRAYER

Father, when all is hopeless, let us find our hope in you.

40 Turning point

As with the seven seals, the final judgment is preceded by an interlude in which we see again the heavenly reality. Here heaven comes down to earth, in the form of a great angel. The spiritual truth which underlies the events of the world is now brought into the world's arena.

The interlude of chapter 7 showed us the sealing of the saints for their protection, and presented them as God's army. The second interlude will show the battle for which they are prepared.

Pivotal passage

The next two chapters mark a turning point in the book. New symbols appear which will be explained more fully in the rest of the work: the beast from the pit, the great city, the conflict between the beast and the Church. The steady progression of judgments is suspended (one more seven-series will come) and is replaced with lengthy expositions of themes.

More importantly the people of God now figure prominently. In fact, as we shall see, it is here that the main message of Revelation actually begins.

Revealing angel

In 1:1, John declares that his prophecy, in typical apocalyptic manner, was given through an angel. So far no revealing angel has appeared to give a message. Now comes 'another mighty angel', establishing a link with the angel of 5:2 who called for someone worthy to open the scroll of God. The angel comes wrapped in the signs of God's mercy; the rainbow of the covenant with Noah (Genesis 9:13) and the cloud and pillar of fire which led the Israelites out of slavery (Exodus 13:21).

In his hand the angel bears a scroll, which is none other than the scroll opened by the Lamb. This point is obscured by most translations, including NRSV, which term it a 'little scroll', suggesting either a scaled-down version of the first scroll, or a different one altogether. The reason is that John uses the Greek word, *biblaridion*, which is a diminutive form of the word, *biblion*, used at 5:1. However, in the popular Greek of John's time, diminutive forms were often used simply as alternative words for the same thing. (*Biblion* is itself a diminutive of *biblos*, the basic word for book or scroll.) The identification of the two scrolls is signalled by John's use of Ezekiel. So far, with digressions and interruptions, he has been following the story of Ezekiel's call in Ezekiel 2–3.

There Ezekiel sees a scroll in the hand of God, and is instructed to eat it. John sees a scroll in the hand of God, but first it must be opened by the Lamb, for Revelation is now concerned with the saving work of Christ, and is mediated by the risen Lord. Once the scroll has been opened (with attendant portents and revelations) it is brought to John. It is twice stressed that the scroll lies open in the angel's hand (verses 2, 8), and John must eat it (10:8) as Ezekiel did. Moreover, so far the content of the scroll opened by the Lamb has not been revealed. Now John is to digest the scroll and declare its contents (10:11). This is the core prophecy of the book of Revelation, and is what is referred to in 1:1.

Word from heaven

So the angel descends from heaven, bringing a word to the world, and straddles land and sea, showing the all-embracing scope of the message of God. God is not concerned only with a minority of believers, but sends out a call of salvation to the whole earth. Judgment may not have evoked repentance, but now comes a message of salvation to all.

PRAYER

Lord, may all hear your word and know your compassion for the whole earth.

41 Word from heaven

As the angel comes down from heaven, John's viewpoint changes. He is no longer an observer from within the heavenly court of God, but is on earth, perhaps on Patmos, to receive his call to prophesy. Such changes should not bother us, since we already know that John is not writing a straightforward story, but presenting a complex set of insights into spiritual truth.

One such truth is that the spiritual reality symbolized by heaven is also to be found on earth. John is not a dualist, one who divides the world into good heaven and evil earth, blessed spirit and wicked flesh. The angel's descent shows again that the plan of salvation is worked out on earth, and the battle against evil is fought in the material world. Therefore the angel's oath is in the name of the one 'who created heaven and what is in it, the earth and what is in it, and the sea and what is in it'.

It is always a temptation for Christians to see their faith as an escape from a world which often seems confusing or intolerable. This, though, is not Christianity, which is about living out the life of heaven, as much as possible, in the present world. The incarnation itself is a statement that the world is the place to serve God; it is God's creation, destined for redemption, and there is no safe 'spiritual' haven into which we may retreat.

A better way

As the angel begins his proclamation, seven thunders sound, giving a message which John understands, but is forbidden to pass on. Presumably this is another series of judgments like the seals and the trumpets. As they affected first a quarter and then a third of the earth, the thunders might well be supposed to affect half of creation. But they do not come to fruition. We have already seen that the series of judgments fail in their purpose of bringing repentance. There is therefore no point in yet another limited, but more intense tribulation. Instead, the angel comes to bring a better approach to the salvation of the world.

For the time of salvation is indeed at hand, as the mighty angel (perhaps Gabriel—'strong—or mighty—man of God') swears. The angel and his oath are modelled on the last vision of the book of Daniel (Daniel 10–12) where the last days are said to come after 'a time, two times and half a time' (Daniel 12:7). This 'half week' of years is characterized by the 'shattering of the power of the holy people' and is very important for John's understanding of the role of the Church, which must witness under persecution. For now, though, it is enough to know that his message is for the Church as it lives in the end times before the coming of judgment. The message is therefore urgent, and its proclamation cannot be set aside because it is difficult or inconvenient.

All this is to happen before the seventh trumpet—a reminder that the vision of the angel and the scroll belongs with the sixth trumpet. It is therefore a call to repentance which is meant to achieve what judgments alone cannot.

Times and seasons

At this point we need to remember again that for John, the end times are the times in which the Church lives. The seals and trumpets are not a historical forecast, but a description of the world as it is. Only the end of each series looks to the future, with its final consummation of God's triumph (verse 7). Therefore, whether in the first century or the twenty-first, the Church lives and witnesses in the time of the sixth seal; the time of the final call to repentance.

PRAYER

Creator of all, give to us your people a sense of the urgency of our mission to all of your creation.

42
Bitter-sweet news

So far, to the inhabitants of the world, God's purposes are hidden. The woes of the world have not been seen as God's call, and remain puzzling tragedies. The consequences of sin have not been a salutary lesson, but a conundrum. The coming victory of God remains a mystery. Yet that mystery must be made clear. In the New Testament, the term, mystery, means some aspect of God's plan, or indeed the whole plan, which is now made plain by the gospel. So just how God intended to bring about the salvation of the world was a mystery which became clear in Jesus Christ.

It is the job of the prophet to make the mystery clear, for as Amos had said long ago, 'God does nothing, without revealing his secret to his servants the prophets' (Amos 3:7). The revealing angel takes up Amos' saying, but changes a crucial word. 'Reveal' now becomes 'announced', which translates the Greek word for proclaiming good news, or the gospel. It is in the proclamation of the gospel that God's plan is conveyed to the world, and his purposes made clear by the prophetic witness of the people of God. From the perspective of the gospel, sense can be made of the judgment of God. Indeed, the message is seen to be far more than judgment. It is the offer of God's grace and salvation.

The gospel calls people to alter their view of the world. It offers another explanation for how things are, and challenges its hearers to test their own world-view against that offered by God. As such it often finds itself in opposition to the values of the world, and is frequently seen as a threat both to individual lifestyles and to systems of government. Any such challenge can expect to be met with opposition and persecution.

Digesting the word

John is told, presumably by the risen Jesus, to take the scroll and eat it. Like Ezekiel, he finds it sweet, for the message of the scroll is one of hope for the world. The actual contents of the scroll are found in chapter 11, where we see it to be a blueprint for the Church's witness in the time of tribulation which heralds the final victory.

Yet it proves bitter to his stomach, for it also carries the message of suffering for the Church, which by its faithful witness is to be the means of bringing the world to salvation. Bitterness is also a sign of the double-edged nature of the gospel message. It is good news, but in the challenge it poses to the world and to sin, it is also a bitter pill to swallow.

Whether bitter or sweet, though, the gospel must be assimilated before it can effectively be preached. The image of eating the scroll is a picture of the word of God becoming a part of the life of the prophet, who in turn shares it with his churches, and through them with the world.

If the gospel challenges unbelievers to change their viewpoint, it does no less for Christians. As the seven messages to the churches made clear, the Church stands in constant danger of being conformed to the world in which it lives (cf. Romans 12:2). The surest safeguard against that is to make the word of God a part of our lives.

Herald of good tidings

John is now equipped with the message of God, and is commissioned to speak a message with universal significance. So far he has been given a message for the churches of Asia Minor (1:11), but now that message is seen to be for the whole world. His prophecy is about 'many people and nations and languages and kings'. The Greek could just as easily be translated as 'to' rather than 'about', but the end result is the same. The message is to go through his seven churches (that is, the Church as a whole) to the whole world.

PRAYER

Let us listen to you, O Lord, and hearing, become proclaimers of your word.

43
The dimensions of the Church

Now John comes to the centre of his book. 11:1–13 is the content of the scroll he has swallowed. This is his message to the Church; God's plan for the mission of his people, and their role in the salvation of the world. The prophecy will be expanded and explained in detail in chapters 12–15.

Preserving the saints

Ezekiel, in one of his visions, saw a man with a measuring rod (Ezekiel 40:3) who measured the city of Jerusalem, as a symbol of its restoration after the conquest by Babylon. John is now given a rod and told to measure the temple of God. Here it is a sign of preservation rather than restoration, an indication that God, who knows every detail of his people, down to the number of hairs on their heads (Matthew 10:30), will keep them safe in the coming tribulation.

Yet safe is a relative term. John is told to measure the inner sanctuary of the temple, but not its great outer court. The temple in Jerusalem had been destroyed in AD70 during the disastrous rebellion of Judea against Rome. Before then it had consisted of a huge outer area, the Court of the Gentiles, which was open to all, and an inner area reserved for Jews. It is this area which is measured, comprising the Courts of Women and of Men and the Holy Place itself.

The temple, of course, is a symbol of the Church. John is not interested in the literal temple, partly because it was long gone, and partly because a literal temple has no place in his vision of the destiny of the saints. So what does it mean to say that the inner sanctuary will be preserved, but the outer court and holy city will be trampled by the nations? The duration of this desecration points to the answer. Forty-two months is once again Daniel's three and a half times (years—Daniel 7:25; 12:7) during which the people of God will be overcome by God's enemies.

In Daniel, this is a reference to the rule of Antiochus IV of Syria over the Jews. Antiochus desecrated the temple, but was eventually defeated, and the temple reconsecrated. For John, Daniel's prophecy becomes a picture of the role of the Church in the world.

The Church is to be kept safe in its core, its inner spiritual being, but the forces of the world will ride roughshod over it in its physical manifestation, its outer being. In fact, the measuring of the temple, and the trampling of the outer area is another image for the truth that was indicated by the sealing of the 144,000 and the martyrdom of the saints in chapter 7.

There we saw that God will preserve the spiritual life of the Church, keeping his people safe in their relationship with him. At the same time they will undergo persecution and suffering for his sake, and will face the martyrdom which will result in their heavenly triumph.

Claiming the victory?

Nowadays we hear a lot about the victory of the Church. There are those who tell us that we should expect success—usually couched in terms of packed pews and fat collections, if only we 'claim the victory' which is ours in Christ. In fact, if a church fails to grow, or even dies out, it is deemed a failure. John's message should warn us to be very careful in our use of such language. The trampling of the temple, based on Daniel's breaking of the power of God's people, points in another direction. The Church may not always, or even often, be expected to be powerful in the worldly terms of number and riches (look at the churches of Laodicea and Sardis). The immediate result of faithful witness is not always growth and plenty. It can provoke a trampling down by the forces of the world. Yet there is a victory, and there is the certainty that nothing can separate us from the love of God (Romans 8:31–39). We must learn to see that victory in God's terms rather than ours.

PRAYER

Lord, let us measure our success not by the world's standards, but by yours.

44 Faithful witnesses

For the same period of time that the world is trampling down the people of God, that is, during the end times which are the history of the Church, God's two faithful witnesses will be active.

The miracles performed by these witnesses remind us of Elijah (1 Kings 17:1; 2 Kings 1:10) and Moses (Exodus 7:19), traditional heralds of the coming of the Messiah (cf. Malachi 4:5). These, though, are not those prophets literally returning, for each shares the characteristics of both. Nor are they another pair of outstanding witnesses (Peter and Paul have been suggested). The clue to their identity is found in their description as olive trees and lampstands.

The prophet Zechariah had seen a lampstand between two olive trees, which stood for the Spirit of God illuminating the rightful king, Zerubbabel and the high priest, Joshua (Zechariah 4). These are all combined in John's two witnesses, to give us figures who stand for kingship and priesthood, and the light of the Spirit. We have already met this combination of images in the royal priesthood represented by lampstands which is the Church. The two witnesses then, are the whole Church. Instead of the seven lampstands of earlier chapters, there are now two, for this is the number of witness. Deuteronomy 19:15 lays down that two witnesses are the minimum number for a valid testimony.

During the time of persecution, then, the world does not have everything its own way. The Church is called to active witness, and will afflict the consciences of humanity with words and testimony to Jesus which flow like fire from the mouths of its messengers.

Heralds of the kingdom

In Jewish tradition, Elijah was expected to appear as the forerunner of the Messiah, and speculation added Moses as another witness to the coming of the kingdom of God.

Jesus applied the Elijah motif to the work of John the Baptist (Matthew 11:13–14), though according to the Fourth Gospel John had denied that he was literally Elijah returned to earth (John 1:21).

It was this messianic claim about Jesus and his forerunner which the Jews found, and still find, so hard to accept. On the face of it, they have the better of the argument. After all, the Hebrew scriptures, the Christian Old Testament, are pretty clear about the signs of the Messiah. He will bring in a new kingdom in which the lion will lie down with the lamb, swords will be beaten into ploughshares and the holy city of Jerusalem will be a beacon of faith to the nations. Gentiles will flock to learn of the true God, and contentment and plenty will be everyone's lot.

The coming of Jesus brought none of these, though to be sure it brought millions of new believers in Israel's God. It also brought a new excuse for war and persecution; the history of Christianity is scattered with crusades, pogroms and heresy trials. Where is the messianic kingdom, if Jesus is Messiah?

Christians have always held that the coming of Messiah is a two-stage process. The incarnation, heralded by the Elijah-ministry of the Baptist, brought Jesus onto the world's stage. There the work of redemption was carried out by his death and resurrection. But the process is incomplete. Messiah must come again to bring the messianic age to fulfilment; and once again, there must be an Elijah to prepare his way.

We, the Church, are called to be that Elijah, that new John the Baptist. Often wrong and misguided, always sinful, but never quite forgetting to cry out in the wilderness of the world, 'Prepare the way of the Lord'.

PRAYER

Father, give to your people the grace they need, that by their words and their deeds they may prepare hearts and minds for the coming of your Messiah.

45

The salvation of the world

Despite the fiery breath and terrible afflictions of drought which the two witnesses bring, their primary purpose is to call the world to repentance. This is signified by their dress—the sackcloth of penitence. But their testimony seems to have no greater effect than the judgments of God.

A great beast arises, which will play a prominent part in the following chapters. Here all we are told is that it successfully wars against the Church and lays it waste. The two witnesses lie dead and unburied in the streets of the great city, while all their opponents rejoice and even exchange gifts. Christmas has come for those who despise the words and works of God.

The city in which the witnesses die is a place of many meanings. It is not literally Jerusalem, for that lay ruined in John's day and he does not see its rebuilding on earth. Jerusalem next appears as the heavenly city. Yet it is Jerusalem in the sense that it is anywhere that murders the prophets of God (Matthew 23:37) and rejects his anointed. It is Egypt in that it is anywhere that imprisons the people of God; and Sodom in that it is wherever the law of God is flouted.

City of God, city of evil

The symbolism of the city is important in Revelation. Cities are where people live together, work together and grow together. They concentrate all that is best and worst in the human race. There you will find the great churches and cathedrals, the art galleries, museums, theatres, cinemas and industries. Human spirituality, creativity and community gather together and reinforce one another. Heaven itself, the very presence of God, will be seen as a city (21:2–4).

In the city you will also find the drug pushers and prostitutes, the child abusers and thieves. There you will find the poor ground into abject squalor and the rich insulated from reality by their wealth. Slums and shanty towns, rubbish heaps which are the food of the poor, the wheelers and dealers, the pimps and the pickpockets. It is into the city that the wealth of the countryside flows, and from which little comes save demands for more.

It is here that the witnesses proclaimed the word of God, here that they prepared for the coming of the Lord, and here that they were defeated and died.

Resurrection power

But not for long. In a joyful parody of the time of persecution their bodies lie for a mere three and a half days, before they rise again and are transported to heaven. Then a final warning judgment falls, and the unexpected happens. The surviving majority (a startling reversal of the usual biblical idea of a small remnant) give glory to God. In other words, they repent and are converted.

This phrase can have no other meaning. In the Bible, to give glory to God is to acknowledge him as Lord. In seeing the Church's triumph over death itself, the words of witness and the judgments of God at last have their effect. The majority of the city's inhabitants declare their faith in the God who at last has brought about their salvation.

Judgment alone cannot achieve this. The disasters of war, famine and disease, of spiritual and physical evil, should point to a reliance only on God. And so they do, but not without a proclamation of the gospel.

Even the words of the gospel itself, attractive though they are to so many, may stimulate only derision, anger and hatred. As they challenge the city of evil, they provoke persecution and enmity. They are seen as unworldly, idealistic, puerile, or whatever.

But when those who proclaim, who declare the judgment and salvation of God, are themselves seen to triumph over death, then the words and the deeds of God strike home. Then there is repentance, faith and the reception of the gift of salvation itself.

PRAYER

Pray for all who face persecution for their faithful witness.

46
Resurrection hope

If 11:1–13 is the main message of the book of Revelation, to which the first ten chapters lead, and which much of the rest of the book elaborates, it may well be a good idea to take stock of the story so far.

John has written his book to the seven churches of Asia Minor, and through them to the whole Church everywhere. The message is that a time of persecution is approaching, and that this time is not to be seen as exceptional, but as the normal experience of the Church.

The Church, by definition, lives in the end times, for the coming of Christ signals the final phase of God's plan of salvation for his rebellious creation. It does not matter whether that final phase of history is only a few months or many millennia in duration. It is not the length of the end times which signal their urgency, but the fact of the coming of Christ. Since the incarnation, God has been the coming one, whose victory is at hand.

In the light of that coming, the troubles of the world, be they natural disaster or the result of human sin, are a call to humanity to place its reliance on God the creator and saviour, and not on human ability or achievement. It is this search for human self-sufficiency which is the root of human sinfulness, and the basic meaning of idolatry—the worship of that which is not God.

The possibility of redemption has been opened to the world by the death and resurrection of Jesus, the Lamb who was slaughtered, and who now shares the worship of God himself. Human destiny now depends on Christ, and the response of the world to him.

The suffering Church

The followers of Jesus have a key role in the world's response, for it is through their witness that redemption is offered. It is the testimony of the Church which interprets the travail of the world as the call to repentance, and which offers hope though faith in Christ. Such a testimony will find itself in opposition to the systems of the world, for they are founded on the human quest for self-reliance, and the denial of God. As a result the Church will find itself caught up in a conflict with those systems, and will suffer persecution and martrydom.

John, in fact, presents us with a picture of a church composed entirely of martyrs. To be the Church is to suffer the fate of the Church's Lord, and to lie dead in the streets of the city that slew the Lamb. Does this mean that John really expects all Christians to be martyrs? Surely not. The language he uses is a vivid metaphor for the dedication to Christ which he does expect of the Church. There are to be no half measures about being a Christian. The Church is called to wholehearted commitment to its Lord, and to bold proclamation of the gospel. Anything less earns the condemnation which was aimed at Laodicea.

In the same way, John probably does not expect a mass conversion to follow on a literal, visible resurrection of martyrs. But the Church's attitude of hope in the face of death itself is its most powerful witness. The overcoming of the fear of death, the denial of death's power to remove hope, is its greatest weapon. So too is the perpetual resurgence of the Church. In various times and places the Christian faith has apparently been stamped out, only to resurface. Resurrection is the cornerstone of Christian faith, and its continuing experience and testimony.

The hope of salvation for the world is the new message which the scroll brings when it is eaten by the prophet, and is the centre of Revelation's message. Hope, not judgment, lies at the heart of the book.

John does not offer a detailed blueprint for the Church's witness, though he will hint at what issues that witness must address. In each age, culture and society, the Church must find its own means of witness. What is not a variable is the loyalty to Jesus which is the necessary presupposition of its mission.

PRAYER

Lord God, give us, by your mercy, such a love for you that you may always be first in our hearts.

47 God takes charge

With the announcement of the three woes (8:13) John introduced a sense of deepening disaster. Yet this disaster was overturned at the second woe, the sixth trumpet. To be sure, it brought torment to the earth, but it also introduced the scroll of prophecy, the testimony of the Church and the repentance of the inhabitants of the great city. The force of the woes began to fade. Now the final trumpet and third woe comes, and all that John records is the victory song of heaven.

In this way he draws out the two sides of the triumph of God. It is disaster for all that opposes him; sin reaps its own reward, and being allowed to run full course destroys itself. But this is not enough. Left to themselves, the forces of evil would be self-defeating, but they would also destroy the humanity God seeks to save. So the other side of the coin is the call to repentance, which through the witness of the church negates the results of sin, and throws open the gates of heaven.

That is what the seventh trumpet denotes. God has won his victory, and for the forces of destruction it is the final woe, as the destroyers of the earth are destroyed. But for the redeemed it is the victory of God's mercy. The woe is not described in detail, for the emphasis has now shifted to the triumph of salvation. We are not yet given any picture of that either. John saves his final vision of redemption for the end of the book. Before then, he still has much to say about the Church's conflict and the nature of evil's defeat. Instead, the end is interpreted to us through the loud voices (presumably of the four creatures before the throne) which hymn the victory.

Triumph song

That final victory is the moment when the kingdom of God swallows up all other rules. Jesus announced the coming of the kingdom and that kingdom was present wherever he was. It was found in his works and preaching, and in the lives of those who chose to follow him. Despite this it was never fully present. For Paul and the early

Christians, the kingdom was mainly found in the future. It was the goal towards which they strove, and the inheritance promised to the children of God. Now the angelic council proclaims its arrival. There is no longer a conflict of different sovereignties, for God is acknowledged by all as the one and only King.

Since the message of Revelation is that God is in charge anyway, it may just seem a bit strange that his ultimate triumph is described as the coming of his kingdom, or rule. It should not, though. There is a great difference between a rule which is joyfully recognized by its subjects, and one which is resisted and contested.

This kingdom is ruled by God and his Messiah, the two who are inseparable, who receive worship together and who reign together. Once again we see John's implicit recognition of the divinity of Christ. The one through whom God brought about salvation is seen in the end to be God himself. This is a strong corrective to the tendency, found both in the early Church and in modern piety, to see God as a judge who has to be placated by the sacrifice of Jesus. The fact that both rule together reminds us that salvation is, from start to finish, the work of God, who 'was in Christ reconciling the world to himself' (2 Corinthians 5:19).

In the same way, Revelation reminds us that the judgment of God is also the wrath of the Lamb (6:16), for judgment and salvation are inseparably linked. To accept the one is to reject the other, and vice versa.

PRAYER

Open our hearts to your rule, O Lord, that at your coming we may be ready joyfully to enter your kingdom.

48 The end of the future

Like the seven seals, the seven trumpets encapsulate all of history, and as the twenty-four elders add their voices to the praise of God, the worship of heaven builds to a crescendo.

It is a climax which signals the end of history, and in a special sense, the end of the future as well. God is hailed as he who was and who is, but no longer as the one who is to come. The future to which the history of the world was moving has arrived, and has met its consummation in the presence of God. God is no longer the goal to which his people aspire, but the continual presence in which they are to live.

Faithful servants

The judgment arrives, and it is first and foremost the time for rewarding the servants of God. As we might expect, these are the prophets and saints, the usual term for the people of God. They are also all who fear his name; in other words, those who repented at the fall of the city and the resurrection of the two witnesses. These are they who gloated over the destruction of the Church, and who sided with the beast from the pit of chaos in its war against the saints. Now, though, like the labourers in the vineyard, they come late to receive the same reward as those who toiled all day.

Interpreters who see Revelation as being itself a book which gloats over the downfall of the wicked (or who wish to do so themselves) tend to miss this point. The real triumph of God is not that evil is destroyed, for evil is self-destructive. His victory lies in the rescue of so many, for this chapter visualizes the salvation of most of humanity.

Answered prayer

At the breaking of the seventh seal, there was silence in heaven, as the prayers of the saints were heard. Those prayers were answered in judgment. At the seventh trumpet, another image is given, of the song of heaven. This too is a response to the prayers of the saints, to the daily prayer of all Christians: thy kingdom come, thy will be done...

The difference between the outcome of the vision of the seals and that of the sounding of the trumpets is found in the faithful witness of the Church. You could say that John provides alternative views of the progress of history. In the first series of seven judgments, we see the course of a sinful world which ignores all warnings. In the second we see the outcome of a world which contains the leaven of the disciples of Jesus.

Destruction destroyed

Once the salvation of the many has been celebrated, the destroyers of the earth are themselves said to be destroyed. The elders' song echoes the themes of Psalm 2, in which the king of Israel, God's anointed, triumphs over the nations. These will include those who do not repent, but the meaning is wider than sinful human beings.

The nature of the destroyers of the earth will become clearer as the book progresses, but we have already been given hints as to their identity. The forces of destruction, the beast, the riders of the first four seals, the wicked city—everything, in fact, which works against the intended destiny of creation—are the true enemy over which God triumphs and against which his followers are called to fight. These are the powers and principalities which include, but are greater than, the sins of individual people. With these opponents gone, nothing hides the presence of God from his creation. So the inner sanctuary of the heavenly temple is revealed to human sight. In the earthly temple of Old Testament times, the unapproachable nature of God was symbolized by the ark of the covenant. This was hidden in the central sanctuary, the Holy of Holies, and was seen only once a year by the high priest. Now the reality for which it stood is revealed for all eternity.

PRAYER

Lord, may our hope in your coming shine as a light to the world.

REVELATION 12:1-6
Cosmic conflict

John has twice taken us up to the end of history, and twice has drawn back from describing it. In the first series of judgments (the seven seals), the Church was assured of spiritual security and ultimate triumph. In the second series, of trumpets, the Church was revealed as the means of bringing salvation to those who would otherwise perish. Now John back-pedals again, to fill out the story of the conflict between the forces of destruction and the people of God. In fact, 12:1—14:5 is a detailed explanation of chapter 11, the contents of the Lamb's scroll.

To achieve this, he uses images which were well known to the world in which he lived. He draws on stock pictures from apocalyptic literature and on a myth which was widespread in ancient times.

The mother and the serpent

In Greek legend, the great serpent (in Greek, *drakon*) Python sought to destroy the goddess Leto because it was foretold that her son would be the slayer of the serpent. Leto was rescued by Poseidon, god of the sea, and gave birth to Apollo, who duly killed Python.

In the Babylonian myth of creation, the sea monster Tiamat was killed by Marduk, the god of light and son of Damkina. The links with the sea are seen in Revelation's dragon, who breathes out a flood of water, calls a great beast out of the sea and like Tiamat knocks a third of the stars from the sky.

From ancient Persia came the story of the dragon Azhi Dahaka, who was fought by Fire, son of Ahura, the god of light. In Egypt, Isis was pursued by the dragon Typhon, slayer of her husband, Osiris. In time Isis gave birth to Horus, who destroyed the dragon.

John's readers would be familiar with at least some of the variations on this ancient pagan myth, and would see the point John was making. The hope of salvation from evil and chaos which such stories embodied has now become reality; a reality known to the Church and shared through its witness with the whole world.

Baptizing the pagan

Some Christians are disturbed at finding echoes of pagan thought in the Bible. Surely pagan things are bad, and biblical ones good? This attitude leads groups such as the Jehovah's Witnesses to ignore Christmas (once a pagan winter festival) and forbid the pagan practice of birthday celebrations.

The biblical writers are wiser. In the God of Israel they see the fulfilment of the hopes of the world, the reality to which the myths of old were shadows and pointers. So Genesis can take the story of the flood, with its affinities to Babylonian legend, and use it as the vehicle for a meditation on sin and redemption. Isaiah can use the story of the woman in labour and the defeat of the serpent (Isaiah 26:16–27) as a picture of God's victory over evil. John can use images which struck chords in the minds and hearts of his readers and through them state the purpose of the people of God.

The point is that the hopes and aspirations of the world are not a threat to be avoided, but a dream which finds its waking reality in Christ. So we celebrate the winter festival (in the northern hemisphere) as the feast of the one who brings light to the darkness of the world, and warmth to hearts locked in the coldness of sin. We celebrate our own birth, for life is the gift of God, and our coming into the world is a part of his work of creation, the opportunity of a life lived in his love and service.

We can read again the myths of the conflict between chaos and order, light and darkness, and know that the struggle has truly taken place. God in Christ has confronted the forces of evil and defeated them through the cross.

PRAYER

Father, open our eyes to the desire of the world for hope, that we might share the hope that is ours in Jesus Christ.

50 Mother of salvation

If John has used a pagan myth for the shape of his story, he has thoroughly baptized it by peopling it with biblical characters. A good analogy that has been put forward is that of a modern political cartoon. For instance, Red Riding Hood and the wolf may be drawn with the faces of politicians. The message is easily understood: one is being represented as naive and trusting, the other as a menace to his career or policies.

So the glorious woman in labour is drawn from Eve, the mother of all (Genesis 3:16), whose offspring will smite the serpent's head (Genesis 3:15). She is the woman who brings forth the Messiah (Isaiah 7:14), and more importantly she is Zion who brings forth a son and many children (Isaiah 66:7–8). In other words, the woman represents the people of God, (she is crowned with the twelve stars of the patriarchs and apostles) from whom comes the Messiah, who will defeat the serpent.

The woman has been seen as Mary, the mother of Jesus, and so she is; but Mary as the representative of the people of God. She has been seen too as the Church, but only if the Church is recognized as being one with the entire story of Israel. She is in fact, the whole historical people of God, whose pilgrimage through the centuries has resulted in the birth of the Messiah.

His story

It is always worth remembering that neither the Church nor the individual Christian, lives in a self-contained moment of time. The troubles and triumphs, temptations and virtues which we experience from day to day are part of a story which goes back to the dawn of recorded time and beyond. Through that time, God has been active in the world, bringing his people to the point where he could become one of them. And he has remained active since then, working out the consequences of the incarnation in the lives and deeds of his followers.

We are a part of that story, bound to it by faith and experience. It is our story which is being told in the symbolism of the woman and the dragon. We have been taken up into the story of God and his Christ, and have become players in the drama of salvation.

Perfectly wicked

Against the woman comes the dragon, with seven heads and seven crowns. Seven, the number of completeness, suggests that this creature is the perfect epitome of evil. It comes as no surprise to find that this is Satan, the devil himself (verse 9). Like the greatest of the beasts which opposed the people of God in the book of Daniel, the serpent has ten horns, the symbols of power (Daniel 7:7, 20). For make no mistake, evil is powerful.

In our day, the devil is out of fashion, and evil itself is doubted. We prefer to speak of fallibility, of misdirected potential. In the face of unreasoning destructiveness, of the negation of creativity, hope and life, we are dumb. Yet the twentieth century alone has seen such evil as to beggar description. Call it the devil or not, it is there and it is strong.

Yet there is one who is destined to break its power, and in the end to defeat it utterly.

PRAYER

Lord, when we are confronted with the reality of evil, keep before us the other vision—of your life and grace, of your goodness and victory.

51
REVELATION 12:4-6
Gospel story

The life, death, resurrection and ascension of Jesus are covered in just two verses. Despite Satan's attempt to destroy him, he evades defeat and ascends triumphantly to heaven. There is no doubt that the woman's child is Christ, for he is to rule the nations with a rod of iron. We have already met this reference to Psalm 2:9 in the letter to Thyatira (2:27) and will see it again at 19:15 when Christ returns in triumph. John, who seems usually to have the Hebrew Bible in mind, deliberately quotes the Greek translation, the Septuagint. There the word for rule is literally, 'shepherd'. Once again we see the ambiguity of Christ's victory. The iron rod may well be an instrument of discipline and wrath, but it can just as well be the defensive weapon of the shepherd/protector. Which it will be depends on the response of the nations, in which the Church's witness will play no small part.

Short story

Why, though, is the subject of the four Gospels condensed into two brief sentences? Firstly, John's intended readers are Christians, who know the story well. It is the foundation of their faith and the reason for their existence. They need no more extensive reminder.

Secondly, the story being told is the tale of God's people and their conflict with Satan. To be sure, the hope of victory and the meaning of their history centres on Christ, but it is their task and calling which is in view.

Defeated dragon

The story of Jesus is portrayed as an escape from the dragon. From an earthly perspective, there was no escape at all. The conflict with evil which began with the temptation in the wilderness ended at Calvary. From the viewpoint of heaven the picture is vastly different. It was through his death that the forces of evil were defeated; a defeat which was made apparent by the resurrection, and leads the Church to worship Christ as the Lord of glory.

Protected people

Meanwhile the people of God remain under his protection. The woman, who disappears from the pagan myth after giving birth, remains the centre of attention. Like ancient Israel, she is kept safe in the wilderness, the place of pilgrimage and meeting with God. This safety is no more a physical protection than any of the other promises of God's protection which Revelation gives. The period of 1260 days is once again Daniel's three and a half times, the time of persecution and spiritual warfare. The image of the woman's nourishment in the desert is a repeat of the sealing of the 144,000 (7:3–8) and the measuring of the inner temple (11:1–2). The spiritual security of the people of God is assured. They cannot be defeated in the ultimate sense, but they can and will know tribulation.

Desert refuge

In the Bible, the desert is an ambiguous place. It is where Israel meets God, but it is also the place of testing. There the Israelites worshipped the golden calf, and complained about God. There God led them for forty years until he had forged a people of faith. It was to the desert that Jesus was led by the Spirit for his own time of testing. The image of God's security is therefore not a passive one. To be kept by God is to be continually challenged and made to grow in faith and devotion. Hence the woman is not merely kept, but nourished. God's security is not stagnation but growth.

PRAYER

Lord, nourish us with your word and your body and blood, that we might grow in faith and grace.

52
The devil's demotion

The account of the child's escape from the dragon is not all that John has to tell us about the significance of the coming of the Christ-child. Just as chapters 12–14 are an explanation of chapter 11, 12:7–10 explains verse 5 and is in turn interpreted by verses 10–12 before the story of the woman and the dragon resumes at verse 13. Once again we see the complex structure of John's writing, with visions within visions within visions, all tied into a whole to present a dazzling message which strives to reach beyond the limits of mere words.

War in heaven

War breaks out in heaven, the devil/dragon and his followers are expelled by Michael, commander of the heavenly host, and come crashing down to earth. The victory, though, is not really that of Michael, even though, as the guardian angel of Israel, he was the most important angel in Jewish thought. The acclamation of victory which follows in verses 10–12 makes that clear. Once again, what John hears explains the significance of what he sees. It is the victory of Christ, shared with the martyr Church, which is the defeat of Satan.

In visionary language, John is describing the consequences of the appearance of the child. Through his death and resurrection, Jesus has conquered Satan's power, and there is no longer any place for the dragon in heaven.

Devil in heaven

The notion that there was ever a place for Satan in heaven strikes us as strange. There are two reasons why it really is not.

Firstly, 'heaven' is the spiritual realm, not the final destiny of the saints and redeemed creation. It is the sphere in which the spiritual significance of earthly events is played out. So it has its dark side. By showing the dragon (identified with the serpent of Genesis 3, the bringer of sin and deceit) expelled from heaven, John is making a profound point. The coming of Christ, and above all his death and resurrection has already scored the decisive victory against the forces of darkness. They are not yet defeated, but any hope they may have of eventual success has been removed.

The second reason for Satan's heavenly presence is found in the evolution of Jewish and Christian thought. Satan means adversary, and in his first biblical appearances, he is part of the heavenly council of God. His job is that of prosecutor of sinners. He is the one who points out human error and demands justice for it (Job 1–2; Zechariah 3:1). In later thought, Satan evolved into the adversary of all that was good.

With the coming of Jesus, forgiveness and mercy rule supreme. There is no longer any place in heaven for one who points up sin, whether out of a desire for justice or from a love of trouble.

Just mercy

We have to be careful, though, to avoid suggesting that Christ's sacrifice somehow acts against the justice of God. The biblical term 'justice, or righteousness, of God' refers more to his faithfulness to his promises than to a concept of legal exactness. Salvation is the work of the one God from beginning to end, as he remains true to his promise of mercy. The one who is to come with salvation is, after all, God himself. Indeed, the work of salvation is in line with God's justice as it is presented in the Bible. God's judgment as it often appears in the Old Testament is assumed to have a bias towards forgiveness. Mercy is always on offer to the penitent, and finds its consummation in the cross of Christ, where the incarnate God bears the burden of human sin on his creatures' behalf.

PRAYER

Lord of mercy, let us never be deceived into thinking we are beyond the reach of your forgiveness.

53

Wings of eagles

The fall of Satan from heaven marks the arrival of salvation and the kingdom of God. This does not refer to the final victory, but to the exaltation of Jesus as Messiah. He is now enthroned in heaven, having struck the decisive blow against sin and evil on the cross. We can tell this simply by the fact that these verses obviously comment on the expulsion of the dragon from heaven by the enthronement of the woman's child in verse 5.

None the less, the cry of praise in heaven has a sense of looking forward to the final coming of God's kingdom. It has been made a reality by Jesus. By his authority the accuser has been cast down, and can no longer charge the followers of Jesus with their sins. The coming of the kingdom is about wiping away sin through the death of Jesus.

Victorious Church

The Church shares in Jesus's victory, and no longer needs to fear condemnation (Romans 8:1). Once again, though, we are reminded of the nature of the Church's victory. The people of God can overcome Satan, indeed already have overcome him by the blood of the Lamb. On the other hand, this overcoming is not the easy 'claiming of victory' which some would lead us to believe. The devil is defeated but not destroyed. He has come down to earth in vicious anger, and resisting him takes the very blood of the saints.

It is by their faithful witness, their refusal to be daunted in the face of death that they triumph. To conquer by the blood of the Lamb is to share his death, and so gain his resurrection.

Heaven, then, can rejoice, but woe to the earth, to both believer and unbeliever, for the fight goes on there until the full total of martyrs has been attained, and the full number of the sinful redeemed (6:9–11; 11:13).

Continuing conflict

Evil has been emptied of ultimate significance by the cross, but its power is still real in the here and now. The dragon falls to earth, and seeks to wipe out the people of God, but she is given eagle's wings to flee into the desert. Since verses 7–12 are essentially a repetition of verse 5 in greater detail, verses 13–14 repeat verse 6, stressing that the people of God are to be kept safe from the spiritual consequences of Satan's attacks during the three and a half years of persecution. The eagle draws attention again to the exodus theme (Exodus 19:4; Deuteronomy 32:11–12), when God bore his people from Egypt on eagles' wings, and fed them with manna.

Unable to shake the true security of God's people, the dragon heads off to make war on the rest of her children. The rest, that is, in distinction from Jesus, for he is the first-born of many children of God (Romans 8:29).

Redeemed humanity

Chapter 12 is dominated by the images of Eve and the serpent, and this gives us a further insight into the nature of the people of God. The woman does not represent merely the Church, nor even all of Israel. She is the symbol of the new humanity which God calls into being through the offer of salvation. The Church has a crucial role in the new humanity, by bringing to faith the many who hear and see its testimony. It can never claim, though, to be all that God will save. As the closing chapters of Revelation will reveal, that number is vastly greater than we may sometimes hope.

PRAYER

Those who wait for the Lord shall renew their strength, they shall mount up with wings like eagles (Isaiah 40:31). Lord, may it be so.

54

The Antichrist

In his war against the˙ saints, the dragon calls forth a pair of allies. Together they will form a blasphemous parody of the holy Trinity.

The first of these allies is a beast which is summoned from the sea; that is, from the waters of the bottomless pit, the place of chaos (11:7). The beast is a composite figure, based on the four beasts described in Daniel 7. Daniel's beasts represented four successive empires of increasing wickedness. By combining Daniel's creatures, John ends up with a beast which, like the dragon, has ten horns and seven heads. It is therefore to be seen as a kind of incarnation of the dragon. It has apparently suffered death, but lives again. The devil's parody of Jesus, it is the Antichrist, the vehicle of Satan in the world. At the same time, its origin in Daniel suggests that it is an empire, followed by the whole earth and acclaimed for its power.

Evil empire

John's readers at this point would surely have recognized the Roman empire. They would have been right. The monstrous power which held the allegiance of virtually all the known world was based in Rome. It called for unswerving allegiance, and even worship. From the Christian point of view, it demanded what could only be offered to God, and so it carries blasphemous names. We are not told what these names were, but they could be found in imperial inscriptions and on Roman coins; the claims of emperors to divinity, and the demand of worship offered both to the emperor and to the spirit of Rome.

This does not exhaust the significance of the beast, however. In chapter 17 we shall see Rome riding the beast. In an important sense, the beast is not Rome alone. Indeed, it is the machinery of worldly power: armies and politicians, oppression, injustice and cruelty. Here is the nation when it sucks its citizens to destruction in war. Here is the ambition of states when they march over the borders of weaker neighbours to bring slavery, oppression and genocide. Here is greed, hitching a ride on the coat-tails of power, looking for opportunities to loot and annexe. It is the city we met at 11:8 and will meet again in Babylon/Rome. With its apparently invincible armies, glittering wealth and universal rule, there is little room for wonder that the whole earth followed the Rome-beast, besotted by its power. Yet, says John, this adulation is nothing less than the worship of the beast's master, Satan himself.

Dangerous blessing

From John's point of view, Rome is the current manifestation of Antichrist, though there were no doubt many Christians, such as those of Sardis and Laodicea, who would have disagreed with him. Rome provided prosperity (for some) and peace, at least according to the Imperial propaganda machine, which extolled the benefits of the *pax Romana*, the Roman peace. John, like other perceptive writers, knew that this was not the whole story. Such peace as there was, was won at the cost of freedom and of enforced conformity. The Roman writer Tacitus gives one of his characters a telling saying; 'Rome makes a desert and calls it peace' (*Agricola* 30:5). Prosperity depended upon acknowledging Rome's supremacy, and above all, its divinely granted right to rule.

How could those who proclaimed the lordship of Christ bow the knee to another divinely appointed lord? How could those who worshipped the living God burn the official offering of incense to Caesar?

Rome indeed offered real blessings, though not as many as it claimed. But the price of Rome's grace was too high for those called to live by the grace of God.

PRAYER

Father, let us not accept the blessings of the world at the expense of knowing you.

55

REVELATION 13:5-10
Undermining evil

The beast makes great claims for itself, and so speaks blasphemy against God, the one true ruler of all. Ironically, it is God who allows it to do so. The use of the passive, 'it was allowed' is a typical Jewish way of speaking of God, originally used because the name of God was too holy to be spoken. It passed into Jewish and Christian writing as an accepted way of describing God's actions.

The beast is seen to be the same one we met at 11:7 which makes war on the Church for forty-two months. No doubt it and its master see this as a sign of their own power. In fact, it is part of God's plan of salvation, where the Church, witnessing in opposition to the Antichrist, suffers the martyrdom which brings conversion to the world.

Temple of God

The beast slanders (the basic meaning of 'blaspheme') and derides the dwelling of God, which turns out to be people who dwell in heaven. This in fact is the Church on earth, whom it wars against and conquers. The image is of the people of God as his living temple (1 Peter 2:5) within whom he dwells. They are physically on earth, and called to serve God there, but their true homeland is in heaven (Philippians 3:20) and in Christ they have a share in that final dwelling even now. In the knowledge of that eternal destiny, they must be prepared to face with endurance and faith either captivity or martyrdom as required.

The authority of the beast is also permitted by God, and for the same reason. Satan may believe (verse 3) that he has imbued the beast with his own power, but in the end, such power is exercised only because it fits God's purposes (cf. John 19:10–11). This raises the question of why God allows such evil to exist. The answer which Revelation presents (and any such answer must in the end be inadequate) is that God *allows* evil to run its course so that he might bring good out of it, and let the evil destroy itself. Such an answer, of course, can only make sense if in the end good will triumph. John affirms that the decisive battle has already taken place on the cross, and that the final consummation will follow in due course.

Eternal plan

The stark choice which is presented between the worship of the beast and of God divides the inhabitants of the world. They are either in the Lamb's book of life, or they devote themselves to earthly power. In the Greek of Revelation, it is the Lamb that was slaughtered from the foundation of the world rather than the names which were in the book from the beginning. NRSV has altered the order of words (which is grammatically possible) in order to bring verse 8 into line with 17:8, which does apply the phrase to the names in the book of life.

We should go with the Greek order, and see here a reference to the eternal nature of God's plan of salvation. The death of Jesus was not an emergency measure, but a part of God's plan from the beginning. Salvation for sinners has always been his intention.

However, in the light of 17:8 we still are left with the uneasy image of a book of the redeemed which appears to have been finalized before time began. At the same time, John is clear that repentance is open to all, for otherwise the Church would not need to witness and suffer. The names in the book of life can be removed (3:5) and in 21:24 the rebellious kings of the earth appear effectively to have been added to the book. The notion of writing in the book before the foundation of the world is not about strict predestination, any more than the Lamb was literally slain before the world began. Both verses (13:8 and 17:8) stress the same point. Salvation is part of God's eternal purpose, that Christ should die in order to offer a way for sinners to return to God.

PRAYER

Father, we do not understand the conundrum of evil, but we trust you to see us through it and to defeat it.

56
False prophet

As if the beast from the sea, the 'incarnation' of Satan, were not enough, another beast arises. This one comes from the earth, which helped the woman against the dragon (12:15–16) and its appearance is far from fearsome. It has horns like a lamb. To a casual glance, then, it may seem helpful and benign. But its voice is a dead give-away.

False religion

By this stage, readers familiar with the sayings of Jesus might well be expecting a false prophet, for the Lord had linked the rise of such deceivers with the appearance of false messiahs (Mark 13:21–22). Indeed, the second beast is henceforth called the false prophet (16:13; 19:20; 20:10). It arranges miracles, and calls the world to worship the first beast. It would take John's readers no time at all to recognize the apparatus of the imperial cult, the state religion with its temples to the genius of Caesar and the goddess Roma. The second beast's miracles reflect some of the gimmickry which was actually used either to impress the gullible or lend drama to the celebrations of the cult. The satanic parody of the Holy Trinity is now complete. The dragon is pretender to the throne of God. The beast which is anti-christ bears the marks of death and resurrection. The false prophet mocks the work of the Holy Spirit by directing worship towards Satan and his beastly manifestation.

The second beast is a deadly threat to the lives of those who do not worship the imperial power. At the time John wrote, persecution was probably slight and sporadic, but when it came, it was most likely focused on the emperor cult. A simple test of loyalty to the emperor was to burn a pinch of incense at his altar. Failure to do so was treasonable. Compliance, though, was a denial of Jesus, the one true Lord.

No doubt some of John's readers thought nothing of such acts of loyalty to the empire. They wanted to be good citizens, they could point to the divine origin of the state (Romans 13:1–7) and to the non-existence of idols (1 Corinthians 8:4). However, this was neither effective witness to Christ, nor spiritually harmless, for behind the glitter of the empire lay the deadly reality of spiritual evil.

There was also a mundane economic incentive to comply with the cult. While there was no literal ban on dealing with those who did not join in the imperial cult, failure to do so could affect one's business. Pagan temples guaranteed trade deals, hosted merchant guilds and formed a deep-seated part of the fabric of society. Withdrawal from that part of life could affect the business interests and the social life of Christians.

There were therefore apparently good reasons for Christians to conform to social and religious expectations. They would avoid threat to their lives, they would avoid social and economic disaster, and they could justify it with a theological argument.

John's reply is to extrapolate the present situation. What will they do if, in parody of the sealing of the saints, the beast demands that all be marked with the sign of his ownership? For that is what it really means to go along with imperial worship. The time to stand fast is now. There can be no compromise with any power which demands the honour that is rightly due to God.

Pressure

Pressure to conform to the world's expectations has always been the Church's greatest temptation. It has often yielded. Discerning the point at which to resist is never easy, but it is necessary (Romans 12:2). Christians must tread a fine line between adapting the gospel to a given time and place and losing sight of it altogether.

PRAYER

Lord, grant us discernment, to know your will and to distinguish it from the demands of the world.

57 The mark of the beast

We have so far ignored one characteristic of the beast which is obviously important to John since he mentions it twice—it has received a mortal wound, but lives. Obviously, this is Satan's mocking version of the death and resurrection of Jesus, but can we say any more than this? The clue to understanding John's symbol comes in the last verse, where the mark of the beast borne by its worshippers is said to be the number of a human being.

Number games

In the ancient world, there were no special symbols for numbers, such as the Arabic system we use. Instead, letters of the alphabet were used, so that a = 1, b = 2, j = 10, k = 20 and so on (or would, if we applied the system to the English alphabet). By adding together the letters of a name, a number could be arrived at which was held to carry a description of the character or fortune of the individual. This process of number substitution is called *gematria*. It so happens that if the Greek form of Nero Caesar is written in Hebrew characters, it adds up to 666. If the Greek word for beast is put into Hebrew letters, it also adds up to 666.

All this may seem a bit far-fetched to us, but in John's day gematria was a popular way of interpreting names, finding correlations between them, and making coded references to people. There is a well-known piece of graffiti at Pompeii, which reads, 'I love her whose name is 545.' The woman in question would know who was meant, but few others would. John obviously expects his readers to recognize the number of the beast. The fact that the number is derived from a Hebrew version of a Greek word is not a problem, since we know from other sources that this sort of cross-language puzzling went on. John probably expected his readers already to be familiar with the significance of the number, even if most of them knew no Hebrew.

Fatal wound

But can we be sure it was Nero? The wound of the beast suggests that it was. Nero committed suicide in AD68, but his death was widely thought to be a ruse. A legend quickly grew up that Nero was in hiding and would eventually return, perhaps at the head of a Parthian army, to reclaim his throne, or to inflict punishment on the empire which had turned against him. (The Senate had declared him an enemy of the people.) This idea was particularly popular in Asia Minor, which had suffered little at Nero's hands, and where he had been a popular emperor.

The death of Nero seemed to have dealt a fatal blow to the empire. It led to the 'year of four emperors' (AD68–69) as civil war broke out in a struggle for the throne. Yet the empire survived and carried on even stronger than before. For John, the myth of the returning Nero becomes a symbol for the empire's ability to survive disaster and come back renewed. At the same time, Nero is a fitting symbol for all that is bad about the beast. Not only was he a tyrant whose excesses were too much for the Romans themselves, he was the first great persecutor of Christians. When rumour attributed the great fire of Rome (AD64) to him, Nero found the Christians a handy scapegoat and executed many with a savagery that drew the sympathy even of the blood-thirsty Roman mob.

The image of the Antichrist, then, is one which can be summed up in a particular individual, but which is far more than one person. In the same way, we speak of Hitler, and thereby encompass all the atrocities of the Nazi régime, whether they were carried out at his direct order or not.

PRAYER

Father, uphold all those of your people throughout the world who face the spirit of the beast, and suffer for their faith.

58

Naming the beasts

If we are right in seeing the beast of Revelation and its false prophet as a system rather than an individual, whether Nero or some other, what are we say about its identity? Was John referring only to Rome? It seems very unlikely, especially in the light of what he writes later, in chapter 17. The beast is any power system which gives itself a status that is due only to God. The second beast is any system of belief and worship which bolsters the claims of the first beast. It is the religious and philosophical justification of injustice, oppression and idolatry. It is the propagandist who speaks reasonable words in support of wrong.

Naming names

Throughout the Church's history, the image of the beast has been used to condemn the opponents of Revelation's interpreters. Protestants have identified the beast with the Pope or the Catholic Church. Catholics portrayed Luther and Protestantism as the Antichrist. Both of these seem equally shocking to modern Christians. Yet similar claims are made today, in both religion and politics. Ronald Regan's description of the USSR as an 'evil empire' drew on the same tradition, while America is described as the 'Great Satan' by Iraqi and Iranian propagandists.

If John's dreadful warning about the beast is to be heeded, it has to be more than a handy school-yard insult. The main characteristic of the beast is that it claims the allegiance which only God can command. That must surely be our starting point if we are to apply it to our own age. Some candidates immediately suggest themselves. We have already mentioned the Nazis. We could speak also of Cambodia's Khmer Rouge régime, and the Stalinist rule of Russia, in each of which the state demanded total control, complete obedience.

These are obvious examples of the beast's modern incarnations. They are also safely distant from the lives of Western Christians. Surely, though, the beast's claims are at times felt much closer to home. An uncharitable newspaper once described a Christian politician as someone who would never let his faith get in the way of his politics. Whether or not it was true in his case, it points up the danger very well. There is a temptation to accept the claims of institutions close to home as reasonable and normal. They need to be subjected to close scrutiny, for quite often they are claiming too much. It is salutary to remember that the beast may seem to be slain, only to rise up again.

Seductive words

If state and society carry within them the possibility of manifesting the spirit of Antichrist, so do religion and ideology. Karl Marx's main criticism of religion was that it was used to give divine sanction to an unjust status quo. So it was, and still is. The most disturbing thing about the second beast is that it looks like a lamb. Even the Church can become the false prophet when it preaches support for the establishment before it preaches Christ. The Church's greatest sin has been when it has allowed itself to be part of the system of government to the exclusion of criticism.

In a similar way, secular ideology speaks the seductive words of the false prophet. In modern culture, it is normal, reasonable and sensible to assume that Christian faith has nothing to offer. The Church and its leadership are portrayed as slightly ridiculous, mostly harmless and quite irrelevant. No good reason is given. It does not need to be—as long as the words of the dragon are heeded, the false prophet has done its work well.

The only cure is to keep our eyes fixed firmly on Jesus Christ, and to follow closely in the steps of the Lamb. To speak out against all that opposes God, and to proclaim the gospel of Christ before all else.

PRAYER

Lord God, 'grant that we may so pass through things temporal that we finally lose not the things eternal'.

59
Holy war

Satan's trinity of evil presents a formidable force. Ranged against them is a greater one. John next sees the Lamb, standing on Mount Zion, the symbolic place of God's presence and salvation (Psalm 2:5–6; Isaiah 24:21–23; Joel 2:32; Micah 4:6–7). With him are the 144,000 who make up his holy army.

Most commentators assume that this vision refers to the final triumph of Christ over the beast. This is unlikely. The Church which stands with him is described as the numbered host of the fighting people of God (7:4–8) rather than the countless multitude of the final kingdom. Moreover, they are the first-fruits—the first instalment of the harvest to follow (see Deuteronomy 26:1–11). Through their witness many more will be brought into the kingdom of God (11:13). This is not a vision of the end, but of the status of the persecuted, witnessing Church.

Heartland

In opposition to the followers of the beast, the people of God are marked with his name. They belong to him, and are safely installed on Mount Zion. They are not literally in Jerusalem, of course, any more than they are literally in heaven. They are all over the world. They are encouraged and buoyed up by a voice from heaven. It is the voice of God which they hear, sounding like that of the risen Christ (1:15) mingled with the thunder of the presence of God (4:5) and the music of heaven (5:8–9). They sing already the song of heaven, though this is meaningless to the world which follows the beast. It is a song which comes from the knowledge of God.

The fact that the praises and the song of Christ's army take place before the heavenly throne is John's way of saying where the heart and true life of God's people lie. In fact, in Revelation, the praises of God always take place in heaven, until heaven and earth are made anew (chapters 21–22).

Like a mighty army

The most misunderstood verse in Revelation is surely the description of the 144,000 as virgins who are undefiled by women. Is the Church really only made up of men? Are women defiling? Hardly. This is an image taken from the regulations for holy war in the Old Testament. Sexual intercourse, while good, was seen as making the participants temporarily unclean as far as participation in worship was concerned. Therefore those who went to fight God's wars were expected to abstain from sex during the time of their holy, military service. John's description of the Church as celibate adult males is purely symbolic, intended to drive home the picture of a holy army. It conveys neither his views on sex nor on women.

While it is an army, the host on Mount Zion does not conquer by force of arms. It conquers by following the Lamb wherever he goes—even to death. Once again, John uses the language of combat to describe the reality of sacrifice. The Church conquers through its willingness to die for Christ.

The conquest lies in the success of its witness, which brings in the rest of the harvest of salvation. That witness is honest and truthful, in contrast with the lies of the beast and the false prophet, for the people of God are blameless. This last word translates a term which can mean both morally upright and physically unblemished. John surely intends the ambiguity. The Church is called to be morally pure, but also to be a sacrifice, if need be—and in the Old Testament, sacrificial victims must be spotless.

PRAYER

Cleanse us by your Spirit, Lord that we may serve you. Open our ears that we may hear your voice, and join in the worship of heaven.

60

Eternal gospel

As a counterpart to the three woes come three angels, proclaiming the gospel which is the weapon of witness wielded by the army of the Lamb. It is a call to recognize God the creator and bow before him in worship and repentance. At the same time it is a proclamation of judgment. The gospel is not an optional extra for those whose religious taste runs that way. It is a stark choice with eternal consequences. All the earth faces the decision of whether to acknowledge God or to follow after the beast.

The beast is now revealed in its incarnation at the time John wrote. It is the great city Babylon, which John's readers would easily identify as Rome. Already Babylon is personified in female form; a picture which will be painted more fully in chapter 17. Babylon, the great imperial power of the Old Testament had become a byword for corruption and evil power. Its destruction can only be good news. The gospel is the good news that God comes to tear down the structures of evil and oppression, and to remove the source of evil's glamour.

Cup of wrath

Babylon does not have the appearance of being entirely evil. She holds a cup from which all the nations have drunk (Jeremiah 51:7). Power, glory, pomp and success make a heady and seductive brew. Why do people choose to reject God? Because the alternative offers real pleasure. No one would ever sin if sin was not enjoyable and desirable. It is in its long-term consequences that it is destructive. Adultery is enjoyable; until it comes to light, and trust and love perish. Power and wealth bring security and pleasure, but at the cost of the security and pleasure of others; and in turn that spells the lessening of the one who has paid such a price.

So the intoxicating brew which Rome offers is also a cup of wrath. The judgment of God is built into sin, and it becomes its own punishment. The destruction of the power of Babylon, then, is the removal of the seducing glamour. The gospel comes to shed a new light on the glory of Rome (and all its successors). In its light, the true picture emerges, and those who have been made drunk have the chance of recovering from their addiction.

If they do not, proclaims the third angel, then they will share the fate of Babylon. Those who have worshipped God will find his eternal presence a blessing and a joy. For those who worship the Babylon-beast, the presence of the Lamb and the holy angels is no joy at all—it is eternal torment.

Verses 9–11 are the most terrible in the book of Revelation. The point of them, though, is not to describe the literal fate of those who reject God, any more than any of the other images are literal. It is to point to the horror of rejecting God's offer of eternal life. The essence of eternal life is a relationship with God (John 17:3). Those who have placed their love, trust and worship in the passing powers of this world have no foundation for the life of eternity.

On the face of it, this is hardly good news. The third angel, though, is merely spelling out the fate which is the alternative to the gospel. The good news is that this need not be the final consequence. The light of the gospel still shines, Babylon is doomed, and her cup may be rejected.

Holding fast

We must not lose sight of the fact that Revelation is a book for the Church. John is aware that the brew of Babylon smells good to Christians too. They must hold firm to the faith, and remember whose mark they bear.

PRAYER

Lord, it's not easy to ignore the lure of things we know to be wrong. Keep us firmly in your grasp when our grasp of you grows weak.

61

REVELATION 14:13-15
The coming Lord

The saints who obey the call to endurance are promised eternal life, in one of the best known verses from Revelation. Verse 13 is often quoted at funerals, where, appearing out of context, it reinforces the popular, non-Christian view that judgment is on the basis of good works. The deeds which accompany the saints into heaven, however, are their acts of faithful witness. In John's vision of total commitment these have led to their martyrdom. The blessedness, or eternal joy, which they are promised is because they have died 'in the Lord'. This is one of Paul's favourite terms for Christians, and here it has the same meaning. It refers to a relationship of faith and love with Jesus Christ.

That faith and love can only be shown as genuine when they flow out in the life and actions of his disciples. As often in the New Testament, John ties together the faith which saves with the works which demonstrate the reality of faith.

At the same time, there is a sense of reward for work well done. The efforts of those who labour to serve God will not go unrecognized.

Being ready

The term, 'labour' is used by Paul to describe missionary work, and has a similar sense in John 4:35–38, where the task of making disciples is likened to a harvest of ripe fields. Verse 13 leads into the first of two harvest images. John sees the Son of man, Jesus himself, seated on a cloud, which indicates the glory of God, and reminds us of the cloud which marked the triumph of the two witnesses who are the church (11:12). The image of a son of man on a cloud is borrowed from Daniel 7:13 where a human figure takes dominion from the beasts of empire. This then, is Christ coming in his final glory and judgment (Mark 13:26–27; 14:62). Yet another of the angels of Revelation appears to relay God's command to him, for the time of his coming is known only to the Father (Mark 13:32).

It is a strange fact that many clever and impressive interpretations of the Bible rely on the ability to ignore simple and straightforward statements. Here John accepts Jesus' own clear word that the time of the end is known only to God the Father. Yet throughout the Church's history interpreters of Revelation have sought to find a clearly documented prediction of the final coming of the kingdom of God. They have taken John's numbers literally, combined them with those of Daniel, Ezekiel and who knows what others, and drawn up detailed schedules as though the Second Coming were being planned by railway timetablers. The strange thing is that repeated disappointment never seems to put off the next clever interpreter.

All this runs in quite the opposite direction from John's meaning. The reason for his call to endurance and perseverance is that the time of the end is not known. The Church must be ready at any moment for the coming of its Lord. The task of bearing witness will not wait until tomorrow because that may be too late. On the other hand, endurance is necessary because the time may yet be distant. All the time of the Church is the last days, and it lives its life in hopeful expectation of the Coming One.

In this twofold emphasis on urgency and perseverance, John is strictly faithful to the teaching of Jesus. None can tell when the bridegroom may arrive (Matthew 25:1–13), for he comes like a thief in the night (Matthew 24:43; 2 Peter 3:10). The task of his followers is to be ready, and to be found at their labours when he comes.

PRAYER

Lord, thank you that we will one day meet you face to face. Until that time comes, let us learn to be your people on earth.

62

Grain of joy, grapes of wrath

The Son of man comes with a sickle in his hand to reap the earth. Then comes an angel who also harvests the earth, this time under the guise of gathering grapes rather than reaping grain. Why the two harvests?

John's source for the harvest image is Joel 3:13 where God's judgment of the wicked is likened to a grape harvest: 'Put in the sickle, for the harvest is ripe. Go in, tread, for the wine press is full. The vats overflow, for their wickedness is great.' John has reinterpreted the two stages of vine harvesting as two harvests which are strongly contrasted.

The first, grain harvest is carried out by Christ in person and its result is not immediately made clear. The second is carried out by an angel who comes from the presence of God (in the heavenly temple). It is trodden, presumably by Jesus as judge, for the use of the passive, 'was trodden' indicates divine action. The second harvest, like Joel's, is one of judgment.

Bloody vintage

The angel who carries it out is one with 'authority over fire', the image of destruction (20:15). The fact that an angel is involved stresses the distance between those judged and the God they have rejected. So too does the fact that the vintage is trodden 'outside the city'. If we have to ask what city this is, the answer must be the city of God. However, the image is drawn from the Old Testament, where death sentences are carried out beyond the boundary of the community as a sign of the expulsion of the offender from the people of God. For the same reason, Jesus was crucified outside Jerusalem, but there is no suggestion in verse 20 that the treading of the second harvest has any saving significance.

The gruesome image of blood flowing for hundreds of miles and several feet deep is one of total destruction. It is 'as high as a horse's bridle'. In fact, the Greek says, 'the horses' bridles', though no horses have so far been mentioned. The reason is that John is using a stock image taken from apocalyptic writings, which he knew his readers would recognize as an image of judgment. They would also know the treading of blood as God's judgment from Isaiah 63:1–6. The grape harvest is the destruction of those who reject God. By distancing themselves from him they find themselves outside the city, in the place of destruction. It is also a universal destruction. The angel swings his sickle 'over the earth' to gather 'the clusters of the vine of the earth'. It is the terrible vision of judgment on a world which has rejected God.

Reaping the earth

At the same time, however, the grain harvest is also a harvest of all the earth (verses 15–16). Yet it is carried out by Christ seated on the cloud which is the vehicle of the Church's salvation (11:12). Moreover, the actual act of reaping is almost never used in the Bible as an image of punishment or destruction (Hosea 6:11 may be the only exception). Threshing certainly is, but this harvest is not threshed; it is merely gathered in. It stands therefore as an image of salvation, and like the judgment, it is a salvation which encompasses the whole earth. It is this harvest of which the saints were the first-fruits (14:4).

John is not really presenting two harvests at all, but giving us two alternatives. The destiny of the earth may be destruction or salvation. Which it will be depends on the response of the peoples of the earth to the witness of the suffering Church. In turn that witness depends on the faithfulness and steadfastness of God's people.

This is an immensely important point. Revelation is not setting out a blueprint for the development of history and beyond. It is declaring that the future remains open to various possibilities, which depend (at least to some extent) on the ministry of God's people here and now.

PRAYER

Father, thank you that the world is in your hands, and for the privilege of being part of your work.

63

Exodus song

The two contrasting images of the harvests dominate the rest of the book. The judgment of Satan, the beast and Rome is the main theme of chapters 16–19. The victory of the saints and the entry of the nations into God's salvation close the book in chapters 20–22. The present chapter prepares us for this by combining the two themes. Seven angels appear with the plagues which will spell final destruction. At the same time, the martyred Church, now in heaven, sings a song which celebrates the salvation of the nations.

King of nations

With his typical method of overlapping images, John first introduces us to the seven angels who will deliver the deadly payload of the seven bowls. We know they are waiting in the wings, but a more joyful vision is presented. The Church, having won its victory over satanic opposition, now stands with the company of heaven, singing God's praises. In the Greek, 'conquer' (verse 2) is in the present tense—they are those who are conquering the beast and so on. The vision is at the same time one of the final triumph and of the present reality of the suffering church. To bear faithful witness to Christ is to be already part of the heavenly host. To be in the Lord (14:13) is to be already sharing in the worship of angels, archangels and all the company of heaven. It is to be already granted a foretaste of the final victory celebration.

The victorious Church stands around the crystal sea, which is now shot through with flames. It is the symbol of chaos, and now carries the flames of judgment, as evil bears within itself the seeds of its own destruction. It also stands for the Red Sea, the barrier through which God brings his people to safety by fire and water. So the assembled martyrs sing the song of Moses, for a new exodus has taken place, and God has rescued his people once again through the decisive act of Jesus, the Lamb of God.

The song of verses 3–4 has no direct quotations from the Israelites' victory song in Exodus 15:1–18, but it is made up of references to other Old Testament passages which deal with similar themes. It is a careful reworking of the song of Exodus 15 using methods of interpretation which were common amongst Jewish scholars of John's day. Like the original song of Moses, it celebrates God's victory over the might of earthly kings. That victory has a very different meaning from destruction, however.

For the God who desires the salvation of the world, there is no true victory in wiping out opposition. The real success lies in bringing the nations of the world to repentance and worship. Therefore God is celebrated as the king of the nations; not their nemesis but their true ruler. All now fear him and glorify his name. This is the language of worship, not of defeat (11:13). Indeed, all the nations now come before their true king, not in grief and terror, but in worshipful awe and reverence because his judgments have been revealed.

Judgments here do not mean the destructive consequences of sin, which still wait as a dreadful alternative. They refer to God's righteous acts, by which he justifies those who turn to him. Above all, they refer to the sacrifice of the Lamb, whose song this is.

In the new exodus, God has not only saved his people, but he has demonstrated his might by drawing all the nations to himself.

PRAYER

Lord, wherever the power of earthly rulers brings fear and
oppression, may hearts be turned to your rule of peace and love.

64
Final plagues

Once again the heavenly temple is opened (11:19) but this time the reason is not to demonstrate the accessibility of God. It shows that God is the author of the doom which is to fall on the earth; the temple is obscured by the cloud of his presence. To be sure, the bowls, like the other judgments, are the result of human wickedness and spiritual corruption. Yet it is God who allows these full play, that they may burn themselves out in self-destruction, and the obliteration of all who cling to them. The plagues which are to come are the wrath of God.

At the same time, there is a positive purpose to this judgment. God is to remake creation, and before the new can come, the old must be destroyed. (No one can enter the temple, the presence of God, until the seven bowls have been emptied.) In John Donne's words, 'that he may build, the Lord casts down'. What is a painful but necessary experience known to all Christians is also the necessary fate of creation.

Safe in heaven?

We have seen the martyr Church singing praises in heaven, and the coming plagues affect only those who have followed the beast. Some interpreters would argue that this should be taken to mean that before the final doom of the world, Christians will miraculously be taken up into heaven to avoid the sufferings of the world. This idea of a 'rapture' of Christians is based on 1 Thessalonians 4:17. However, it is never mentioned in Revelation, and Paul's purpose is to reassure his readers that all Christians will be reunited at Christ's return. There is no hint in the Bible that Christians will ever be spared the consequences of living in a fallen world.

We need to remember that John is not interested in providing a chronological picture of the end times. The song of Moses and the Lamb is part of the alternative to the plagues—salvation of the nations as a preferred option to their destruction. Whichever it is to be, the Church is called to be in the thick of it, serving Christ and witnessing to his saving grace.

The final plagues affect only the worshippers of the beast because they are a symbol of the results of rejecting God. They are no more a literal description of how the world will end than is any other image in Revelation.

Realism

At the same time, there is a realism to John's depiction, despite the fantastic setting. Like the earlier plagues, these reflect what actually happens in the world. The first four especially, reflect and intensify the effects of the seven trumpets. Whereas the earlier seven-series were limited in their scope, giving time for repentance, the final seven are unlimited, and the image is of universal devastation. Since all ended with the final judgment of the world, we are given a sense of increasing urgency in the face of the troubles of the world. They may lead, with the witness of the Church, to repentance, or they may not. The seven bowls show what happens in a world which adamantly refuses to acknowledge its creator.

PRAYER

Father, as we live in a world of turmoil, give us the faith to see in the suffering around us the birth pains of your new creation. Give us strength to witness by word and deed to your truth, and to see your love and goodness amongst the sorrows of the world.

65
Nature in torment

The voice of God gives the command for the final onslaught, and the bowls are emptied. The first four strike at the created world, and echo the plagues of Egypt. For all their disastrous consequences, these terrible events are the precursors of the new exodus, as God prepares the new creation as the promised dwelling of his people.

The world's disease

The plague of sores marks those who have the sign of the beast. What had been seen as the symbol of security and power turns out to be the symptoms of disease. The trust in something other than God is revealed as illusory.

In fact, all the plagues are symptoms of the world's disease. It is a spiritual illness which springs from the desire of human beings to be their own god, not realizing that by doing so they are worshipping something far worse.

The seas and the fresh waters become fetid blood, in ironic punishment for those who have themselves shed the blood of God's people. At last the martyrs are vindicated, and call from the altar that God's judgment has shown itself to be just.

The heat of the sun becomes unlimited, and is no longer the source of life-giving warmth, but of punishment. The end result is not repentance, as it was at the fall of the city (11:13), but rejection of God. Instead of giving him the glory, the afflicted curse God; they choose not life, but death (Job 2:9).

Eco-disasters

It is a mistake to suppose that John is aiming to make literal predictions of future events. By the same token, it is foolish to try to relate specific aspects of his prophecy to particular events in a given age. However, it is equally foolish to try to pretend that what he has to say must apply to someone other than ourselves. He paints a picture of a world turned deadly by the results of human sinfulness and pride.

It fits our present age perhaps more closely than any other.

We are rapidly coming to realize that the human race is part of a vast and delicate system which we have the power to uphold and nurture or to destroy. The biblical images of humans as the caretakers and gardeners of creation (Genesis 1–2) stand in stark contrast to the way we treat the world. Through pride and power, high technology pollutes the sea and the fresh waters with chemical effluent, sewerage, radioactive waste and excess fertilizer. It strips away the delicate protection of ozone to let the sun scorch human skin. It tears the earth's atmosphere-making forests apart to make way for hamburgers on the hoof. Meanwhile the poor and dispossessed cut down the same trees for fuel, allowing farmlands to erode. They crowd into shanty towns where disease takes daily toll and add to the burden of the earth's pollution. Technology creates its own untreatable diseases, and antibiotics create resistant germs for which there is no cure.

In the face of such disasters, we often hear the word 'apocalyptic'. It fits well.

This is not to claim that we live in imminent expectation of the end, or at least no more so than at any other time. It is to claim that Revelation's picture of a world which brings disaster on itself by ignoring the creator, and the very fact of creation, with all its attendant responsibility, is grounded in reality, and not in fevered imagination.

PRAYER

Lord, we mistreat what you have made and suffer the consequences because we do not acknowledge that you have made it. Open our eyes to you, the creator, that we might see your creation and take our proper place within it.

66 Glamorous darkness

Darkness, another Egyptian plague, continues the exodus theme. It is also symbolic of the continuing irony in God's judgment. Those who have lived in spiritual darkness under the rule of the beast are condemned to it forever, and find it to be a torment. Still there is no repentance, but only blasphemy, for these are the ones who have given their souls to the blaspheming beast, and there is no room left in their hearts for repentance.

We frequently say that it is never too late to repent. In this world at least, that is surely true. We have to recognize, however, that repentance comes less and less easily to those for whom sin has become habitual. There comes a point where light is too painful for those who dwell in darkness even to contemplate (John 3:19-21).

Defiant forces

The sixth bowl looks almost out of place. Instead of bringing suffering and destruction, it allows the forces of the world to regroup. But of course, it is disaster. The forces of the east reflect the same Roman paranoia about the armies of Parthia as we saw in the four horsemen of chapter 6. It also carries ideas of the myth of the returning Nero. Most of all, though, it is from the east that the armies of Babylon and Assyria marched on Israel. These are the forces of chaos and destruction.

Instead of repentance, the armies of the world take to the field. No doubt they do so under proud banners, beating the drums of patriotism and just warfare. They are ready to fight for their homeland, their way of life and their friends and families. Above all, they sharpen their swords in the name of religion, spurred on by words of prophecy and the sight of miracles. Faith is a great incentive to death. For that is what it is. The hidden force behind their battle preparations is demonic. They have worshipped the beast, the force of military might, the apparatus of statehood. They have listened to the false prophet, and now it calls on them to make the supreme sacrifice. The devil has his martyrs too, and they look like crusaders.

Their death does not lead to eternal life, for it is not offered in glad sacrifice to the truth, but comes in the attempt to bring destruction on others.

It is a glamorous delusion, but a powerful one. It has seduced Christians into the belief that faith in the God of love and sacrifice can be spread by the sword and the rack, the stake and the gun. So the voice of Christ breaks in. This is Jesus as he spoke to the seven churches, calling them again to be awake, to be clothed in faith and righteousness, lest they be taken in by the false prophets and bogus messiahs (Mark 13:21–22).

Last battle

The forces of chaos take their stand at Har-magedon, 'the mountain of Megiddo'. The town of Megiddo was the site of several major battles and so is a fitting place for conflict. However, it is in a plain, and while the nearest mountain is mount Carmel, the site of Elijah's confrontation with the prophets of Baal (1 Kings 18:20–40) it is not really close enough to be known as the mountain of Megiddo.

John is probably characterizing the site of battle as a mountain to symbolize the beast's parody of Christ. As the Lamb and his army stand on mount Zion (14:1), the beast's army stand to oppose them. In the Old Testament, the sacred hills ('high places') of Canaanite religion came to symbolize false worship, and were a constant temptation to worship other gods. The 'mountain' of the kings of the east is the mere might of the world's corrupt systems and can offer no eternal security and no hope of victory. Hence their mountain has no real existence. Like the emperor's new clothes, it exists only as a delusion to fool the gullible.

PRAYER

Father, there is a real attractiveness to the promises of evil. Give your people clear sight, that they may walk only in your ways.

67 The weight of judgment

Unlike the first two seven-series, the bowls contain no interlude between the sixth and seventh judgment. The picture of the heavenly reality in which the Church shares is now complete. All that remains is to describe the coming of God's kingdom in its fulness. For that to happen, the destruction of the sinful systems of the world must be brought to completion.

City of evil

The seventh angel pours out the bowl which signals Satan's downfall. The air, the area of the heavens below the moon, was held to be the sphere of the devil's influence (Ephesians 2:2). Now that region is judged, and the voice of God declares the completion of the victory which was won by the cross of Christ (see Jesus' cry of 'it is finished'—John 19:30).

The great city, which is Babylon and Jerusalem, Egypt and Sodom, is destroyed by earthquake. This is effectively the same earthquake as we saw at 11:13. There it only destroyed a tenth of the city, while here its ravages are total. It is still the same one because it is not a literal earth tremor, but includes the response to God's judgment. In chapter 11 there was repentance. Here there is not, and destruction is total. Once again we are presented with the alternative outcomes which spring from the gospel's call to decision.

The cities of the nations fall with the great city, for they all partake of it. All cities embody to some degree the corruption of Babylon, and in so far as they share its characteristics, they must share its fate.

The fate of the cities also embodies an economic and political reality which John will explore more fully in the next two chapters. Those kingdoms and cities which have tied their fortunes to that of Rome cannot stand when the central pillar of the empire is removed. In preparation for the next section, Babylon is mentioned again by name and singled out as the recipient of God's wrath. All cities share in the great city, but Babylon/Rome embodies it most fully. Babylon is made to drink the cup of God's wrath, for it has made others drink its own cup of corruption (14:8).

The cup/bowl image is a recurring theme in the later chapters of Revelation, and helps to tie it together, forming another of the strands which would aid John's readers in understanding the structure of the book.

Final destruction

Like the sixth seal (6:14) the seventh bowl removes all hiding places and destroys all the false security of the world. The mountains may also symbolize false religion, like the mountain of Megiddo. There is no refuge in misdirected faith, no safety in the isolation of islands. All stand exposed to the wrath of God, which falls like a ton of bricks—or a hundred pounds of hailstone.

The tragedy is that it need not be so. It is open to people to acknowledge God, to turn away from their own insecure bastions of faith and power, and be accepted. Instead, they curse God.

In a lesser way, we see a similar choice in daily life. Sometimes in the midst of affliction, a person may find God, and with him the strength to cope, and the compassion of a Lamb who also suffered. Yet others may look for strength in bitterness and rejection: 'What has God ever done for me?' John calls us to the first option. He does not promise an avoidance of suffering; far from it. He offers a share in the life of the Lamb that was slain.

PRAYER

Lord, teach me to seek you in the darkest parts of life, and so become a beacon beckoning others to your light.

68
Beautiful evil

As the seventh bowl brought final doom to the sinful world, special mention was given to Babylon, the city that sums up all evil. Now, as it were, the camera zooms in closer for a detailed look at the fall of the great city. In actual fact the destruction of Babylon is simply described by the angel. What John sees is the city in all its glory. She looks like a whore.

There are three figurative women in Revelation. The first we have already met, the woman clothed with the sun. She is the people of God, through whom God enters the world in Jesus Christ, and she is kept safe by the power of God. The third is the bride of Christ who is both the first woman transformed, the people of God as they yet will be, and the city in which God dwells. The second, the harlot Babylon, is the devil's counterpart to the others. She is a people and a city, and she is dressed so gloriously that even John is amazed.

Occasionally, readers of Revelation assume that John's use of female imagery for Rome/Babylon reflects his view of women. It does not. In the ancient world, cities were commonly characterized as female, and John is simply using the stock images of his time, and of the prophetic tradition in which he stood. The image of the city-harlot has a long history in biblical imagery (Tyre—Isaiah 23:16–17; Nineveh—Nahum 3:4 and, above all, Jerusalem herself—Isaiah 1:21).

Rome the seducer

The woman of chapter 12 was kept safe by God in the wilderness. In the Bible the wilderness is also the place of temptation, so it is there that John is taken in his Spirit-given vision to see the whore. She is certainly tempting. Overdressed in the richest clothes and jewels, she is the picture of the costliest courtesan. She offers pleasure and delight, the opportunity to forget the cares and responsibilities of everyday life. No wonder that the kings of the world (and their subjects with them) have given themselves to her. Drunk in her embrace they have indeed forgotten. They have forgotten the God who calls them to responsibility before him, who demands their worship and offers them everlasting love.

Sexual promiscuity or unfaithfulness is a standard image of idolatry, the basic sin of turning away from God and offering his due to something that is other than him, and therefore cannot be worthy of it. Rome, the great ruler of the world's mightiest empire, seems to offer much, but has taken even more. She has demanded the worship due to God, she has removed the dignity of nations and people who should stand before God as his responsible servants. She has removed their freedom and their worth.

She is therefore not only Rome, but all cities which suck their inhabitants into a culture which has no room for God, and demand a compliance which leaves no space for the free service of the creator. She is not only the seducer of kings; she is the bright goal to which the poor and desperate flee, only to be swallowed up. She sums up all that is evil in the city, and so represents in a mystery (that it, a symbol visible to those with discernment) all cities and nations which rebel against God and practise idolatry.

Violent temptress

Babylon may be a seducer, but she has no soft words for those who reject her blandishments. The people of God who stand against her are murdered, because for all her allure, she is still founded on the power of violence. Hence she is seated on the beast which represents the military might of the empire and the power of naked strength. Her beauty is a velvet glove over the iron fist of the legions.

PRAYER

Father, look with mercy on the cities of the world, that they may discover how to reflect the bride, and not the whore.

Mysterious beast

John is amazed, presumably at the beauty and magnificence of Babylon. He should not be. Evil, as we have seen before, is beautiful and attractive. Its beauty lies in the fact that it is almost always a perversion of something good. Fornication and adultery are wrong, but they are a wrong use of the bright gift of sex, which itself is good and beautiful. Wealth and prosperity are not evil, for they bring comfort and security, and the ease which is necessary for the growth of culture. Yet they come at the cost, all too often, of the suffering and poverty of others who have as much claim on comfort and security as the wealthy. It is not wrong to celebrate one's homeland and culture, to be proud of the traditions and self-identity of one's nation. Yet we can all too easily see the way in which nationalism and tribalism spill over into contempt for others, and a belief in the right to conquer and subdue.

The angel therefore explains the glorious harlot by pointing to the beast on which she rides. It is here that her power is found, and it is this naked oppression which has made her the whore she is.

The sleeping beast

In a parody of God and his Messiah (4:8), the beast is described as the one who was, is now, and is to come—but its coming is to defeat, not to victory. Perhaps there is also a warning here to those who see little sign of the beast on their horizons. The churches of Asia Minor may well have responded that the terrifying, anti-God power which John ascribes to Rome is hardly matched by the reality. Nero did terrible things to the church in Rome, and there may have been sporadic acts of persecution elsewhere, as at Pergamum when Antipas was killed. Now, though, for those with a little discretion, things are hardly so bad.

For those of us today who live in relative freedom, in lands where Christianity is respected or tolerated, the bestial picture of the state belongs to another age. We put across our point in polite debate and have our say in the democratic process.

John's answer is that the beast does not die so easily. It does not disappear with the death of Nero, the defeat of Hitler or the flight of Idi Amin. It is always ready to rise again, for it lies sleeping in the very structures of the world in which we live. In fact, it *is* those structures, which are never purely good, even if they are rarely purely evil. All too easily they may change, the balance of justice may tip, and the beast run free once more.

The sixth emperor

John sees his churches as being poised at the threshold of the beast's reawakening. The seven heads of the beast represent seven kings (and hills, just to make the identification with Rome quite clear). Five have gone and the sixth is now reigning.

Many commentators have seen this as a sure way of working out exactly when Revelation was written. All we have to do is decide which of the preceding emperors are the five who have fallen. It is impossible. There were five emperors before Nero, and Nero is already in the past.

In fact, the seven emperors are symbolic. They are the total, complete list of the rulers who will hold sway before the end comes. John's churches are in the time of the sixth simply because they are in the end times, waiting for the return of Christ and the beginning of the great tribulation. All churches, at any period of history, stand in the time of the sixth emperor.

Like all the references to the imminence of the end, the list of emperors is a call to the churches to be ready for their coming Lord. The corruption of the empire in which they live is itself a sign of the end times. There is no place, no time for complacency and compromise.

PRAYER

Give your people open eyes, Lord, to see the beast even when it appears to sleep, and to bear witness against it.

The difficult and complex explanation of the beast in verses 9–14 has been a fertile ground for all sorts of strange theories. For those who see Revelation as a coded description of the course of future history, the heads and the horns have been seen as world empires and coalitions of nations, including even the European Union. Verse 9 suggests that the meaning is one which John expected his readers to know, which rules out a 'literal' futuristic interpretation.

In fact, he is once again using the myth of the return of Nero. There were two forms of this idea. According to the first, Nero was in hiding, but would return to reclaim his throne and take the empire on to greater glory. This is the form of the legend that lies behind chapter 13. There the beast parodies the resurrection of Jesus by surviving a mortal wound and carrying on. The mythical Nero is seen as the one who typifies the beast's ability to return from the dead.

A second version had Nero returning at the head of an army to wreak destruction on his faithless empire. This is the form of the myth which John is using in the present passage. The beast itself is one of its own heads, which is both one of the seven and yet an eighth. In other words, Nero, a fallen emperor whose time appears to have passed, returns as an extra and final ruler, who embodies the nature of the beast itself. The coming of this ruler spells the end, the destruction of the beast.

John's readers were familiar with the Nero legend in both its forms and would recognize the images he was using. In chapter 13 the return of Nero formed a handy symbol to show how the secular power apes the resurrection by appearing indestructible. Here in chapter 17 a version of the myth which has the emphasis on judgment is brought into play. The beast has not only a mocking form of resurrection but also its own second coming for judgment.

That judgment, though, recoils. Those who give their allegiance to the beast, who place their trust only in earthly might, will find that their names are not in the book of life which represents God's eternal desire for the salvation of his creatures (verse 8). They may have set themselves up as the world's arbiters, but discover that they themselves are judged by the Lord of lords and King of kings.

Historical reality

John is doing more than playing with images. He is presenting a powerful analysis of the Roman empire and of secular power itself. The whore who is Babylon is sustained by nations and peoples whose ambitions and hopes cannot be thwarted forever. They will want their turn at the top. In the end, the empire must fall, torn apart by the subjects whose strength she milks for her own ends.

Nero will return, turning the power of subject armies against Rome itself, and tearing down the glorious edifice which is built on fear and oppression. An empire which is built on injustice and power will eventually fall prey to the very forces which sustain it. Of course, there is no literal Nero. The point is the instability of a rule based on injustice. If naked power is the way to rule, than anyone can seize that power. So John envisages the subject nations, the ten horns, turning against the rider of the beast and consuming her.

Judgment comes

All this is part of God's process of judgment. He has given up his opponents to the results of their own chosen way, and they destroy themselves. They may believe that they are seeking to further their own ends. In fact, they have fought against Christ and his saints, and through the self-destructiveness of evil, the Lamb has prevailed.

PRAYER

Lord, open the eyes of the rulers of the world to your rule, that they may turn from the way of force and discover the rule of your kingdom.

71 The state of the beast

Chapters 13 and 17 of Revelation, the images of the beast which serves Satan and wars against the people of God, give one of the most radical criticisms of the state in the Bible. The beast represents the military might of Rome, and reaches beyond that into a timeless representation of all secular authority and power. As such, it appears to stand in direct opposition to those biblical passages which have formed the basis for most Christian political thought.

Servant of God?

For Paul, writing to the Roman church, the state was God's servant, expressing his desire for order and good behaviour. It wielded the power to punish transgression on behalf of God himself (Romans 13:1–7). This view is echoed in 1 Peter 2:13–15. For the author of 1 Timothy (whether Paul or not), the rulers were those who provided the peace in which a godly life might flourish (1 Timothy 2:1–2). In the Old Testament, the state of Israel and the people of God are effectively indistinguishable, and even pagan kings may unwittingly carry out God's purposes (Isaiah 45:1–7).

In Revelation there is no mitigating view of the state at all. To be sure, the beast, like its master Satan, ultimately falls into God's plan, but only in a negative way. It promotes no good, and is the opponent of God rather than his servant.

Redressing the balance

It has been argued that John's pessimism is the result of the situation in which his churches found themselves. We have seen, though, that there was no widespread persecution at the time of Revelation's writing. Perhaps the memory of Nero's bloodbath was sufficient to remove any rosy view of the state from Christian eyes, or at least from the less complacent, more perceptive, prophetic vision.

John's analysis, however, runs deeper than that. Paul had already hinted at limits to the goodness of the state. By characterizing it as the servant of God (Romans 13:4), he had used a term which in the Old Testament carries the weight of responsibility rather than privilege. John sees an empire which promotes the worship of false gods, and rewards wealth to the detriment of the poor. The whore Babylon is dressed in the most expensive finery. It is a city for the rich and powerful, but not for the downtrodden and despairing. It seeks to control the distribution of wealth (13:16–17) and is the arbiter of human worth.

It is no accident that the two churches which receive uncritical praise, Smyrna and Philadelphia, are notable for their poverty and powerlessness in worldly terms (2:9; 3:8). Their very weakness has prevented them from being sucked into the system of the beast.

John's judgment of the state, then, has two main components: the false worship it promotes and the unjust society it embodies. Paul's implicit criticism, which is overlooked by most commentators on Romans, is made the focus of John's picture. His viewpoint redresses the balance in the biblical view of secular politics and provides a warning for all who would seek to promote a Christian political understanding.

A truly biblical view of secular power will indeed seek to see, and to foster, the state's service to God. It will look for that which promotes well-being and good living. But it will seek to see signs which point to God as the true source of salvation and it will seek justice and equality for all.

Above all, it will never be complacent. It will never mistake even the best earthly society for the kingdom of God, for beneath the surface of any state, the beast slumbers lightly.

PRAYER

Encourage our prayer, Lord, for those who rule, and above all for justice based on the knowledge of your love.

72 Luxury and desolation

The prediction of Rome's destruction at the hands of the very forces which have raised her to greatness might seem to be the last word on the city which has brought so much misery and sin to the world. John has not finished, however. 18:1—19:8 presents a dirge for the death of Babylon. It is a song of lament modelled on the doom songs of the Old Testament prophets, where the fall of the city is foretold in the form of a song of grief written as though it had already happened. John borrows from prophetic laments over Babylon (Isaiah 13; Jeremiah 51), Tyre (Ezekiel 26:1-6), Edom (Isaiah 34) and Nineveh (Nahum 3).

By using these diverse sources, John reinforces his conviction that Rome embodies all the evils of the infamous cities of the past, and allows us to see her as the embodiment of the wicked city which may be manifested anywhere, in any age. He does more than simply borrow; the song is a masterpiece of prophetic poetry in its own right, and sums up all that calls for God's judgment on the city that has opposed him. It is not simply a triumphant gloating over the downfall of wickedness. It presents a detailed analysis of what is wrong with Rome. It has, in fact, been termed the most trenchant critique of the Roman economy to come from the time of the early Roman empire.

Desolation

An angel shining with the glory of heaven announces the fall of Babylon. In earthly terms, there was nothing to compare with the splendour of the great city, and it has seduced many to false worship. Yet it is nothing to the glory of heaven which is promised to the saints, and in which they have a share already, through the life of worship and prayer. The glory of heaven stands in opposition to the splendour of earth, and it proves to be the lasting glory. The brilliance and wealth of Rome now lies desolate, with unclean beasts and spirits lurking in its ruins.

The demons, perhaps, are those which once were worshipped

as gods in the temples of the empire (Deuteronomy 32:17; 1 Corinthians 10:20). Now their followers are gone, the rich offerings rotted, and nothing remains but haunted desolation. It is worth noting that in the New Testament, while demons and their satanic ruler are taken seriously, they generally seem to lack power without human vehicles. Once cast out of their hosts, they are mere haunters of the desert (Luke 11:24–26). Even Satan himself operates through human agencies, summed up in Revelation as the beast and the false prophet. The point is that we confront the demonic in the institutions and actions of everyday life, not in some abstract world of the 'spiritual'.

Luxurious lies

Babylon seduced the rulers of the world by the offer of power, and drew in the wealthy by the promise of riches. Those who were powerless may have been forced to worship the beast simply in order to survive in a world dominated by the power of Rome. Those with wealth and strength have followed her willingly, ready to seize the opportunities of privilege, 'the power of her luxury'.

Luxury is, of course, the sign of power. It is the powerful who can afford what is unnecessary, and it is frequently gained at the expense of what is necessary for others. In the modern age, we hear much (though unhappily to little effect) of the impact of the wealthier nations on poorer ones. Coffee and carnations are the main exports of nations which desperately need to grow food for consumption at home. But wealth lies abroad, and the power of wealth dictates what will be grown, rather than the needs of the growers.

Rome too sucked luxuries out of the lives of its subjects, creating a life of splendour for the powerful and rich. In return, the true riches of heaven were ignored, and so judgment falls.

PRAYER

Lord, open the eyes of the wealthy to the needs of the poor. Open our eyes.

In the world, not of the world

The doom of Babylon will be shared by all who share in the life of Babylon. So a voice (presumably of an angel, since it refers to God in verse 5) tells the people of God to leave the city, lest they share its fate. The image is borrowed from the return of the exiles in historic Babylon (Isaiah 48:20) and from the exodus theme which runs through Revelation. Does it mean a literal removal of the saints from contact with the sinful world? Many have taken it to mean that, and the Church's history is littered with the stories of sects who have declared themselves separate from 'the world'. There have been those who have attempted to build their own towns and nations, unpolluted by Babylon. There have been those who have lived in secular communities, but built separation into their religious and social lives. Examples of both still exist, drawing their inspiration from the present passage and others such as 2 Corinthians 6:14—7:1, which breathes a similar air to Revelation.

It is unlikely that John is thinking of physical separation. For him, the witness of the Church is carried out in the streets of the city itself, and it is there that martyrdom awaits (11:8). Paul too, explained that his talk of separation was a moral and spiritual refusal to identify with the existing system of values. It was not a call to live lives bounded by the borders of a ghetto (1 Corinthians 5:9–10; 7:29–31). The separation which should mark the life of the Church is a separation of morals and spirituality. This makes it all the more difficult to achieve. It is easy to be a devout and faithful follower of Jesus while singing a rousing hymn on a Sunday morning. It is another matter to make a choice between a football ticket and a charity collecting tin on a Saturday afternoon.

Challenging heaven

Such choices are the stuff of Christian witness, and they are rarely clear-cut. Yet if there is no difference between the lives and values of

Christians and that of the city in which they dwell, then Babylon has indeed triumphed.

Its triumph is temporary, though. The achievements of the great city may indeed be towering, but like the tower of Babel (Genesis 11:1–9), it is an edifice of sin, challenging heaven to act.

Judgment comes, as the city receives the treatment it has meted out to others, and in double measure (Jeremiah 16:18).

Call for judgment

The voice which began with a call for the moral and spiritual separation of the saints continues with a call for vengeance on the wicked city. This is not addressed to the people of God. Their role is suffering witness, not judgment. Despite all its violent and military imagery, Revelation never calls on Christians to take up arms against the evil power. Christian opinion is divided over the question of pacifism, and any discussion of it must take into account the whole of scripture. There is, however, no support for violence in Revelation.

The call for judgment is therefore possibly aimed at the beast and its ten horns of chapter 17, or more likely is a general command to all the powers which combine, willingly or otherwise, in bringing the judgment of God to fruition. In this sense, it paradoxically does include the people of God, for the proclamation of the gospel is itself an act of judgment. Those who hear the word are given an insight into their own situation, and so may choose either darkness or light (John 3:19–21).

However this may be, the judgment of God brings about a great reversal. The harlot who called herself a queen is suddenly a widow; the status which was proverbial for its powerlessness and poverty. Like all earthly riches and good fortune, her position can be overturned in a single day. Her self-sufficiency is not sufficient at all.

PRAYER

Father, we so often unthinkingly accept the way of the world in which we live. Give us a critical faith, that we may know when to accept the world, and when to resist it.

74 Self-pitying mourners

The voice from heaven continues its prediction of judgment against Rome. (Although the speech marks end at verse 8 in NRSV, they are not in the Greek, and there is no good reason to suppose that the angelic announcement ends before verse 20.) The city will not go altogether unmourned to its doom. Three classes of people will raise a lament: the kings who shared its rule and luxury, the merchants who grew rich trading in its luxuries, and the sailors whose livelihood was in the transport of its commodities. God's judgment is couched in terms of economic disaster, for it is the economy of Rome which embodies its wickedness.

Loveless lovers

The kings of the earth join in mourning at the loss of the might of Babylon. Yet the suggestion is not that they mourn the city for itself. They are those who have identified themselves with its idolatry (fornication) and who have shared in its riches. The doom of Babylon spells the end of their own wealth, the loss of their luxuries. Hard times are ahead, and the sorrow is for all they have lost.

The city has encouraged its hangers-on to seek their own gratification and enrichment. It has therefore earned no love for itself, but only fostered a love of wealth, which in the end is a love of self. It has encouraged selfishness, and so is left with no true lovers, but only paid customers who see the whore's death as a loss of their own pleasure. The essence of sin is that it turns in on itself, seeking neither God nor anyone else.

Mingled with their sorrow and self-pity is fear, which causes them to watch from as far away as they can. They do right to fear, for the judgment of Babylon is also the judgment of those who have shared her lifestyle and power.

Self-destructive sin

Just who are these wailing kings? At first glance, they may be thought to be a different group from the kings who, symbolized by the beast's ten horns, bring about the downfall of Babylon by their own attack on her. It may well be that John envisages Rome as being destroyed by invaders. On this view the ten horns of 17:7, 12 represent the surrounding nations which eventually rise up in judgment against Rome, led by the returning Nero. But the fact that the horns were on the beast which the harlot rode makes our earlier view, that Nero returns to raise the subject nations against Rome, a better option. Of course, it could be that since John is quite happy to mix up his images, the beast is no longer in view, and the subject nations are here merely spectators of the destruction.

It is more likely that these are indeed the very nations which have destroyed Rome. Turning on their former provider in an ever greater lust for wealth and power, they have destroyed their own corrupt benefactor, and now see their ambitions go up in smoke. Like so many who have set out on a course of destruction and self-aggrandizement, they stand appalled by the consequences of their selfish actions. They are appalled, though, not at the fate of Babylon/Rome, but at the self-destruction their actions have wrought.

PRAYER

Father, the pursuit of self-interest often damages others, and ruins ourselves. Give to all who suffer the consequences of their own actions a desire for repentance and forgiveness, and a concern for the needs of others.

The second group which will mourn the passing of Rome will be the merchants. Once again, it is self-interest which weeps. The city which rode the beast has none who truly mourns for her; at least, not within her own sphere of influence. The loss the merchants have suffered is immense. Their great cargoes of luxuries and bulk necessities were worth uncountable sums of money. The merchants weep indeed! For in one hour (the refrain for all three mourners—verses 10, 17, 19) their security has been swept away. There is a greater security, one which will last for eternity, but it has been ignored for the illusory safety of wealth and prestige.

Hungry city

The list of the goods which will no longer be traded in is worth looking at. John has provided an accurate reflection of the sort of materials which flowed into Rome by sea. Gold and silver from Spain, precious stones from India, pearls from the Red Sea and the Persian gulf, fine linen from Egypt and silk from China (though its source was unknown to the Romans), purple and scarlet dyes from Asia Minor, are just the start of the list. Fine woods, materials for artisans, spices, all were the epitome of expense. In Rome itself, the wealthy vied with one another in their pursuit of expensive furniture and clothing, the elaboration of their cuisine and the brilliance of their jewellery.

All this represented a vast flow of money from Rome, but little of it went to the people of the empire. The wealth garnered from the subjects of Rome went into the luxuries of her ruling classes.

Only towards the end of the list do normal foodstuffs make an appearance, and even then their mention is barbed. The oil and wheat consumed in vast quantities by Rome itself indicate the dependence of the great city on the production of its empire. The city consumes but does not produce.

The very last item is a telling one. The Greek literally says, 'bodies and human lives (or souls)'. 'Bodies' was a common term for slaves. John has presumably added the rider that these are indeed human lives. The empire deals in people as commodities, along with clothing and livestock.

Weapons of trade

John is doing much more than condemn conspicuous wealth. The trade of Rome was one of its weapons of oppression. There were those throughout the empire who benefited from it. Merchants and rulers did very nicely, thank you. Those who produced the goods which were consumed by the city saw little of the profits. The lot of peasants and artisans was not significantly improved by the immense consumption of the imperial city. In fact it was quite the reverse. As in the modern world, the demands of the consumer dictated what was produced, rather than local needs. Imperial tax and imperial trade worked in the interests of the rulers, but little trickled down from their coffers to the common folk of the empire.

There were few, though, who saw this. The dazzle of Rome blinded the poor as well as the rich. The imperial cult encouraged the view of Rome as divinely favoured, the imperial propagandists promoted a worshipful view of the benefits of Roman rule, and a popular belief in ineluctable fate discouraged thoughts of changing the status quo. For instance, the institution of slavery, which for John is the crowning sign of economic and moral corruption was never questioned, save by a radical Jewish group, the Essenes—and Christians such as John himself.

PRAYER

Father, there are still those who treat people as commodities, as units of trade or consumption, production or resources. Help our world to see people as your great treasure, infinitely loved, and divinely desired.

76

REVELATION 18:14-19
Idolatry and justice

The importance of John's criticism of Roman economics can be seen by looking at the structure of the threefold lament by the kings, the merchants and the mariners. If we were to take out verses 11-14, we would be left with three short dirges sung by those who will 'stand far off' and ending with the refrain, 'in one hour...' (verses 9-10, 15-17a, 17b-19). John has broken into this pattern with an extra section on the disastrous trade of Rome, showing that this is a major reason for the coming of God's judgment.

Soul thirst

The worship of luxuries is a form of idolatry. The exotic fruits and dainties which were the hallmark of privilege had become the focus of their souls' longing. Where the Psalmist longed for the spiritual refreshment of the living God (Psalm 42:1), the heartsickness of Rome's élite turned to the next morsel which might titillate the jaded palette.

The economic sins of Rome are driven home as her dress is once more described (verses 16-17). It is her wealth that has made her a whore, and she has sacrificed honour, integrity and life itself in the pursuit of further riches.

Sailors' lament

The third group to mourn the passing of the city is the seafarers. Ship-owners, captains and hands alike see the passing of their livelihood. The vast commercial fleets which bore the life-blood of Rome are no longer in business.

Most of the sailors would hardly be wealthy, yet they too praise the great city for its unique majesty. The seductive splendour draws rich and poor alike to worship.

Every city

John grounds his visionary foretelling of the judgment of God in a realistic assessment of the economics and politics of his day. Amidst the strange creatures and celestial portents is a keen awareness of the sins of the imperial system within which he and his churches are called to live and serve God.

By making Rome into Babylon, the archetypal wicked city, John demands that his readers look at their own city, their own political, social and economic system. There they will be able to see both signs of the grace of God, and traces of Babylon. The temptation to believe that Revelation is concerned only with Rome, or the first-century church, is denied by this use of universal symbols.

At the same time, we have to resist the temptation to make naive equations. John's condemnation of Rome's imports does not mean, for instance, that all international trade is sinful. On the other hand, we cannot assume, simply because our present economy makes no use of slaves, or that empires are no more, that all is well with our present world.

Trade is still a powerful force for maintaining inequalities in the world. International loans, import tariffs, and diversity of producers work today to ensure that the poorer nations remain poor, and the weak remain powerless.

PRAYER

Father, uphold and strengthen those who work in our world for the spread of justice, for fairness to the weak, and mercy to the poor. And give to us who consume the produce of the world, an awareness of the true cost of our luxuries.

Sad justice

In contrast to the mourners, the angelic voice exhorts the people of God to rejoice at the ending of the harlot's reign.

Many of John's readers would be tempted to wonder what they had to rejoice about. The churches of the trading cities of Asia Minor would contain many who were involved in the empire's commerce. They would find it only too easy to identify with those who mourned the fall of Babylon. Which is no doubt what John intended.

He challenges his readers to ask where their heart really lies. Are they servants of Christ, soldiers of the kingdom who stand against the injustice and idolatry of the beast? Or are they victims of the harlot's seduction, so caught up in the values and promises of the corrupt world system that they can no longer divorce themselves from it? Is the longing of their hearts met by the love of God, or is it slaked by the material promises of the passing age?

Rotten foundations

Those who belong to God look on Babylon and rejoice at its downfall, for they can see beneath the glitter to the reality. In the foundations of the great city lie unspeakable sins. Economic oppression through the merchants who maintained a stranglehold on the empire (verse 23c), and the ruling system's bewitchment to idolatry (verse 23d) have been made perfectly clear in this chapter. There are other things to be taken into account, though.

The harlot has drunk the blood of the people of God (verse 24a; 17:6), for she can brook no opposition. There is no room for those who question her ways, and God's ways are a continual challenge to the world. She has made war on the followers of Jesus, and must answer for that.

Persecution of the Church by no means exhausts her violence. The empire exists by conquest and the rule of the legions. Local rebellion and dissension were punished by extreme measures, and so Babylon is charged with the death of 'all who have been slaughtered on earth'. The charge may be extreme, but then, Babylon is not Rome alone, but every state, past and future, which builds its power on the corpses of its victims.

So God's justice is called down by the victims of Rome, but also those of Britain, in Africa, India and Australia, where 'natives' were obstacles to the path of empire. Justice is demanded by the natives of North America, by Aztecs and Incas (and in turn by the victims of those empires). It is demanded in this century by Jews, Serbs, Bosnians, Croats, Cambodians, Vietnamese...

As the angel hurls his symbolic millstone, it would seem there is little to mourn at the passing of Babylon.

Silent harps

Yet strangely enough, there is. Judgment may seem long overdue, but when it falls, it will silence the musicians and the lovers, the craftsmen and the millers. Have these deserved their fate? Perhaps not individually, but they are caught up in the system which seduces humanity away from God. They have dwelt in Babylon, choosing it over the city of God, and so their beauty and their art vanishes into darkness.

There is surely a note of sadness here. Not at the ending of evil, but at the loss of what could have been. There was real beauty in Babylon, but it was used not for the praise of God, but for the adornment of corruption. Yet, despite the words of the earthly mourners, which are laments for their own loss, the only sense of loss at the death of the great city comes from the one who pronounces judgment on her. God allows human freedom, even the freedom to reject him. But it is still a defeat of his love, and a sorrow in his heart.

PRAYER

Thank you, Lord, for your justice and your sorrow.

78

Witness

In his call to faithful witness, John has been careful not to provide a detailed check-list of how that witness will be carried out. We know that it leads to persecution and even martyrdom. The Church is called to be faithful to death itself, and it is in seeing the triumph of Christians over death that the world's hope of salvation lies.

At the same time as he refuses to give instructions on how to bear witness, John does provide very good pointers as to where that witness will be brought to bear.

Evangelism

In those sections of the modern Church where 'witnessing' is rightly emphasized, there will be little doubt of what John means. Witnessing involves telling others about Jesus, as believers chat about their faith, answer the questions of the curious and make a defence against the scornful.

It will also include more structured evangelism: the setting up of opportunities to hear the gospel in small groups, by home visiting and by street evangelism. All these were practised by the early Church, and John would no doubt be familiar with them.

They are good and important, but fall short of John's understanding of what it means to be a witness to Jesus.

Soldiers and servants

Along with his emphasis on the role of the Church as God's witnessing army, we have seen a detailed condemnation of the forces which oppose God. They are the idolatry, violence, injustice and exploitation which characterize the social, political and economic system which is the beast, and the city of Babylon.

Once these two ideas are put together, it becomes clear that witnessing to the truth of God involves active opposition to the forces of corruption in the world. The Church is called to witness by modelling an alternative view of community, with an alternative set of values; love, worship, equality and justice. This is what it means to be called to separation from Babylon.

That separation of values will go hand in hand with exposing the corruption and injustice which masquerades as reasonable and necessary. True witness will include the struggle for justice and the demand for equality. It will not be content with the explanation that the world must be as it is, for it has seen a better vision in Jesus Christ and his kingdom. It will expose the oppression which is inherent in much international trade. It will point up the injustices in societies which see widening divisions between rich and poor as being natural and good.

Keeping faith in its place

This 'implied text' of Revelation will be as uncomfortable to some modern readers as it would have been to John's first hearers. Many of us have been taught that there is a world of difference between 'spiritual' matters and the 'secular' world. The task of faith, it is said, is to inspire and motivate people in their daily lives, but not to challenge the nature of those lives. This is simply untrue. That was the task of the state religion of Rome, and from time to time the Church has succumbed to its lure. But the very reason why Revelation can brook no compromise with the beast is that the lordship of Christ reaches into every corner of life, and questions the allegiance of every aspect of living. The people of God bear witness to him in everything, or in nothing.

PRAYER

Father, you call us to be your faithful witnesses. Give us courage to witness to your saving love, and your call to justice and compassion.

79
Hallelujah!

There is another response to Babylon's fall. Heaven rings with the praises of God. In chapter 4 we met the four creatures, the elders and the great multitude who form concentric circles around the throne of God. Now a liturgical hymn of praise moves like a Mexican wave from the multitude (verse 1) to the elders and the creatures (verse 4), is answered from the throne (verse 5) and bounces back to the multitude (verse 6). The voice from the throne is not identified, but it is probably a fair assumption that it is Christ's. He shares the throne of God, and receives worship with him, but is still the mediator of worship, which is offered to the Father, through the Son.

It is a constant command to 'praise God', both in Hebrew ('Hallelujah'—verses 1, 3, 4, 6) and Greek (verse 5). Interestingly, this is the only New Testament passage to use the Hebrew word, hallelujah, which was preserved in the Church's worship as a liturgical term. It occurs here probably because John sees this song as echoing the so-called 'Hallel psalms' (Psalms 113–118) with their refrain of 'praise God'. They were sung in the temple at times of pilgrimage and celebration.

Grim vengeance?

To some commentators, the song of praise is a grim sequel to the appalling scenes of destruction at the fall of Babylon. The apparent exultation over death and destruction seems to be a far cry from the Christian values of love and forgiveness. What is being celebrated, however, is not the destruction of rebellious people, but the end of a *system* which has opposed God and has itself brought about the destruction of its followers. God has now acted to clear away all obstacles to the vision of divine glory.

To be sure, this is indeed vengeance for the deaths of his saints, but it is first and foremost the revealing of his salvation. The necessary removal of opposition, of judgment on sinful Babylon, is the other side of salvation. God has waited a long time for the repentance of the world through the witness of his Church (6:11).

Now salvation is revealed, and judgment with it. God's vengeance is never a petty reaction. This is no ancient despot indulging in a fit of rage. It is the God of justice at last declaring that the time has come for the final reckoning.

A major argument in theology is whether God can allow any of his creatures to be lost. Surely anything other than the salvation of all is a defeat for his love and power? The other side to this argument is that love demands a limiting of power. If God creates people truly to be free agents, they must have the power of defying him to the end. In loving, God chooses not to overpower his creatures, even though it ends in their destruction, and his own pain. If John thought in such philosophical terms (and he surely did not), this would seem to be his approach.

In a grim counterpart to the incense of heaven, the smoke from burning Babylon ascends for ever, a statement of the finality of God's judgment.

Just God

The conflict which many see between the mercy and justice of God is a false one. It arises because we tend to think in legalistic terms, of transgression and punishment. On this view, forgiveness is simply deciding to overlook sin. The question then becomes, why overlook sin in some, but not others?

The biblical perspective looks at relationships. Forgiveness is not simply what God does; it is part of an overall process of reconciliation, in which a mutually loving relationship between God and his people is restored. Judgment, then, as we have frequently seen in Revelation, is ultimately the consequence of refusing a relationship with the source of eternal life.

PRAYER

We praise you, Lord, for your justice, but even more for your love.

80 Pre-emptive worship

Heaven's song of praise ends with a declaration of God's reign, and declares the arrival of the marriage feast of the Lamb. These have not actually taken place yet. To be sure, God always reigns, but John has not yet brought us to the point where that reign is universal and undisputed. It stands ready to come, but is still future.

Similarly, the banquet of the kingdom, which Jewish and Christian thought expected as the victory celebration of Messiah's coming has not quite arrived. The people of God stand ready to be united with their Lord, like a bride awaiting her husband, but he is not yet here.

This touches one of the central aspects of worship. When we join to praise God, we do so not only for what he has done, but also for what he will do. Much of the Church's liturgy is a celebration of promise. At baptism we thank God for a person's new birth in Christ, but only time will actually tell whether they will go on to live a life of faith. In the celebration of the eucharist, we thank God for all the benefits of Christ's death and resurrection, though final salvation still lies in the future.

Like Revelation's heavenly worshippers, we feel it is inappropriate to put conditional clauses into worship: 'we praise you God, that you have delivered us from the powers of darkness—provided that we do indeed put our faith in you, and everything goes as it should....' It is inappropriate because there is a sense in which worship reaches beyond the present moment to claim not only the promise, but the reality of the future. Worship lifts God's people into the timeless presence of God, where the marriage supper is not a distant promise but a present reality. The eucharist is both a foreshadowing, and a (no doubt diluted) present experience of the final victory feast.

Self-examination

This is no doubt why John is told to write down the rather obvious beatitude on those who are invited to the marriage feast. The Greek makes it plain that the reference is to those who have not only received the invitation, but have also responded. As Revelation was read out in the worship of the churches of Asia Minor, it would come as a call to self-examination. Have you indeed responded to the invitation? Are you here to receive the blessing of God? Are you indeed one of the faithful witnesses who hold fast to the testimony about Jesus Christ?

So when John falls in worship before the glorious angel who speaks to him, the rebuke is aimed as much at his readers as at him. Whom do you truly worship? You must worship only God, for he alone is worthy. Similarly, the gospel you preach must be only the gospel of Jesus, brought to life amongst you by the Spirit of God. Any other revelation, even if it came from an angel, is false (Galatians 1:8).

Divine Christ

The term, 'angel' does not actually occur in the Greek of verse 9, but it is obviously implied. John's rebuke is entirely consistent with Jewish and Christian thought. Worship may never be offered to anyone other than God, even to an angel whose appearance streams with glory. This makes it all the more significant that worship in Revelation is offered to Jesus. There is a clear division between the divine receiver of worship and all his creatures. Jesus stands on the divine side of that division.

Once again we see the almost trinitarian linking of God, Jesus and the Spirit in verse 10. John and the angel are both servants who worship God and bear witness to Jesus in the power of the Spirit. From the earliest days this has been the centre of the Church's worship and mission.

PRAYER

Praise you, Father, Son and Holy Spirit, for you have redeemed us from the world and promised us your kingdom.

81 The coming of Christ

Several times we have been brought close to the coming of Christ and the final moment of this age. In the sixth seal (6:12–17), the seventh trumpet (11:15–19), the two harvests (14:14–20) and the seventh bowl (16:17–21), we have arrived at the end of history. Each time we have backtracked as John showed us in ever greater detail the conflict in which the Church is involved as it seeks to bear witness to Jesus before the nations of the world.

The final moment arrives. There is nothing more to add, and from now on we will gaze into an eternal future beyond the bounds of history. We are taken back, in effect, to Harmagedon, where the forces of the Antichrist, the beast who embodies the sinful systems of the world, wait for the final conflict with God.

The first vision, though, is of a rider on a white horse. It is Christ, coming in glory as he has promised. Behind him stream the armies of heaven, the faithful witnesses (14:1), dressed in the white robes of victory. He wears many crowns, for he is the Lord of lords and King of kings, whose rule far surpasses any dominion claimed by the seven-crowned dragon.

Suffering king

He has his titles written on his robe and his thigh, for all to see, and he is acclaimed as Faithful and True. He has promised that his rule will come, that evil will be defeated, and his people vindicated. Now he comes to put those promises into deeds. Yet for all that he has a name written on him, it is insufficient to sum up his true being.

In the ancient world, it was held that a name embodied a person's true nature. Jesus is indeed faithful and true, the ruler of all. Yet these are not all that he is. He has a name that only he knows, for his true being lies far beyond human comprehension. Having told us so much, John cannot state the name, but there is a strong clue. When Moses met God at the burning bush, he asked God's name. 'I am who I am' was the reply (Exodus 3:14). God is the self-sufficient being, the one who alone can fully know what and who he is. Jesus too has a name and nature which only he can comprehend. If we want to hazard a guess as to that secret name, it is surely the name of God.

He comes in the white robe of a conqueror, but that robe is dipped in blood. Some commentators see this as the blood of his enemies (Isaiah 63:1–6) but in this vision the winepress has not yet been trodden (verse 15). The blood is surely his own, shed for the sins of the world. We have seen that as the martyrs shed their own blood, they wash their robes in the blood of the Lamb (7:14) as they share in Christ's sufferings (12:11). Now John shows us the original blood of redemption. The one who comes as conqueror and as judge has first shed his blood to be the Saviour.

Victorious judge

Although much of the imagery of this vision is of conquest and military might, it is no more than imagery. Jesus comes not to fight, but to judge, and the weapon he wields is the word of judgment, the sword from his mouth. The victory is that of truth over deceit, not simply of great power over lesser might.

The judgment will be pronounced on the nations of the world. They have followed the beast, and been seduced by the whore, rejecting the witness of the saints and the offer of salvation. Now they are left only with their own pride and power. It will not be enough. Once again he is pictured as coming to rule (literally, 'shepherd' with a rod of iron—2:27; 12:5). If only the nations had repented, it would have been the shepherd's crook.

PRAYER

Lord, as we look for your coming, may we proclaim your saving death in our worship and our witness.

82 The last battle

The final conflict begins with a grisly invitation to the carrion birds. The coming of Christ is the prelude to the marriage feast of the Lamb, the celebration of salvation. The invitation to the birds is a ghastly parody of the heavenly banquet; another great supper of God.

It is only at this point that we catch sight of the beast and his armies. The vision of Christ has captured the eye and rendered the great power of the world irrelevant.

Anti-climax

And then it's all over. No gargantuan struggle, no last minute rallying of the beleaguered forces of heaven for one final victorious push. None of the heroic trappings of mythical conflict. The last battle turns out to be no battle at all. It is simply judgment. The beast and the false prophet are captured and thrown into a burning lake. Their followers are wiped out by the sword of Christ. The armies of heaven do not lift a finger, for they have already won their fight, in the long struggle of the martyrs against the beast.

All the army language is imagery, after all. This is not a battle, but a judgment. There is no literal beast, or lake of fire. What is happening is that Christ pronounces his judgment on the military and political systems of the world, and they are destroyed. There is no place in the kingdom of God for corruption or for oppression. It spells an end to the rule of fear, the favouring of wealth and power, the inequity of trade between rich and poor.

The kingdom brings to a close a system of values based on what people do or have. They are no longer judged on what they make, on their 'contribution to society', on their faithfulness to the party line, or any other of the myriad ways in which we are tempted to judge our fellow human beings. All that is left is the single question: have they given themselves body and soul to the way of the world, or have they reached out in desperate trust to the open hand of God?

False prophet

With the political and social structures of the world go the ideologies and propaganda, the religious justification for idolatry and rebellion against God. The beast from the land (13:11), the false prophet, also perishes in the flames. The call to worship that which is less than God cannot survive the burning vision of the coming of God himself.

It remains true in this present age, that the best argument against false religion is to present the best example of true worship. Faith which results in changed lives, reborn hope and renewed relationships presents a vision of God which overwhelms the lesser gods, be they those with an overt religious claim, or the petty gods of materialism.

House on sand

For those who have invested their very selves in the values and structures of this world, there is nothing left. They have built their lives on a foundation without strength. The word of judgment is spoken, and the sword of the rider mows them down.

To say that this world is a preparation for the next is a cliché. But then, clichés are born because they are true. Revelation presents a consistent call to decide between what is offered by this world, and what is offered by God. To follow the beast is to have no foundation on which to build the life of heaven. Without that, would heaven even be recognized as such?

PRAYER

Lord, give us such a vision of you that when the time comes, we will recognize you gladly.

83
Millennium

Probably the most puzzling section of Revelation is 20:1–10, dealing with the thousand year reign of the martyrs with Christ (the 'millennium'). More has been written on it than on any other section of the book. Basically, there are four ways of approaching the passage, and three of them have been given technical names which describe the view-points of those who hold them.

Premillennialism

'Premillennialism' is the oldest way of interpreting the text, and is sometimes called 'chiliasm' from the Greek for 'thousand'. ('Millennium' comes from the Latin for 'thousand'.) On this view, the passage follows in a simple narrative from chapter 19, and the Second Coming precedes the millennium, which is a literal rule of Christ over the world, prior to the last judgment. It is a period of peace and prosperity in which the newly resurrected Christians run the world under the authority of Jesus. There are several variants of the general idea, but these need not concern us.

To make matters more complicated, there are some who hold a premillennial view (or believe that John did), but suggest that it need not really be taken literally.

Postmillennialism

On this interpretation, 20:1–11 is a separate vision, more or less re-telling the tale of chapter 19. It adds the idea that as the gospel spreads throughout the world, a period of justice and faith develops, which will last for 1,000 years (or at least a long time, since the number may be symbolic). Then comes a final period of rebellion and tribulation, followed by the coming of Christ and the last judgment.

This view allows an optimistic picture of the results of the Church's witness, and gives hope to those involved in the struggle for justice in the present time. However, it fits poorly with the over-all message of Revelation, and few hold it today.

Amillennialism

This is 'a-' as in no millennium, which is rather misleading, because in fact the millennium is held to happen, but is seen as going on now. The reign of Christ is a present reality, and the saints share it with him. The resurrection of the martyrs is a reference to their 'born-again' status as Christians, and Satan is bound by the preaching of the gospel. The millennium is therefore the period of the Church, and is apparent only to the eyes of faith.

This view owes much to the teaching of the great theologian, St Augustine of Hippo, who advanced it as a counter-measure to the overenthusiastic behaviour of premillennialists.

Pure symbolism

The most recent approach, which is truly 'amillennial' in that it regards the passage as pure symbol or metaphor, suggests that like much of Revelation, none of the passage should be taken as a literal description of what will happen. The purpose is simply to make an important theological point—that the martyred Church will be vindicated, and seen by all to be blessed by God. The point here is that John did not intend a reference to any specific events in the history of the world. This interpretation allows us to see that many of the unanswerable questions raised by more literal views are pointless.

This is more or less the approach we will take. The passage is symbolic, offering encouragement to believers.

PRAYER

Lord Jesus Christ, whether there will be a future reign on earth or not, open our eyes to see you reigning now, in our lives and over the world.

84
Binding Satan

Following the victorious return of Christ, an angel is sent from heaven to bind the dragon. Here the devil is given all of Revelation's titles for him: he is Satan, the devil, the dragon, the great serpent. It is as though John wants us to see the full force of the power of evil. The force which opposes God is not to be taken lightly. As Satan, he is the accuser of God's people, the one who points out their sins and proclaims that such have no place in the kingdom of God. As the devil, he is the personification of evil, the focus of all malignity. The dragon, the archetypal monster of chaos, is the opponent of all that stands for order and creation. He is that which seeks only to destroy and finds his strange fulfilment in the ending of all things. The serpent is the tempter, the one who brought sin into Eden and turned humanity from its first intended destiny.

Evil is no paper tiger. It must be faced as the great and terrible force it is. Yet in the end, the dragon is seized by an angel of God and almost contemptuously disposed of. Cast into the pit, the abyss of chaos, he is triply imprisoned: bound, locked and sealed away. Great though evil may be, it is nothing in the face of God. All its despair, destruction and corruption is unable to quench the life-giving force of the creator.

Satan unbound

Why, though, must Satan be released for a time? Why must there be more destruction? In fact, there will not be. Christ has returned, and judgment awaits. The binding and release of Satan are John's way of stating two important truths. Firstly, even the forces of evil work God's will. He does not wish them, but since they are there, they will serve his purpose. They must be tolerated as a painful consequence of human freedom. As long as the world remains in its present state, evil is a possibility which is all too often realized. Yet it may drive people into the loving arms of God, and stand as a permanent warning of the dreadful consequences of rebellion.

Secondly, for these same reasons, evil is resilient. It can never be truly locked away. There is no way of papering over the cracks. Sooner or later, no matter what good resolutions, no matter how just a society, human beings may make, evil will return. In this world, all our victories over it are temporary. They are real and good, but the final abolition of sin can only come when the world itself is remade and humanity enters fully into the life of the new creation. So Satan will run free again, to perish entirely in the new world which has no place for him.

Strong man preaching

Although here the temporary binding of Satan lies in the future, the image is probably drawn from present experience. According to Jesus, it was in his ministry that Satan was bound (Matthew 12:29). He is the strong man who is rendered helpless by the coming of the kingdom, and whose goods are plundered. So he stands by helpless whenever the gospel is received in faith, and sinners freed from his power. Similarly, it was the preaching of the disciples which Jesus saw as casting Satan out of heaven (Luke 10:18). It is the liberating power of the gospel which binds Satan now, and what is now visible only to the eye of faith will one day be apparent to all, as Christ returns in majesty.

PRAYER

Father, it is hard to believe in the triumph of good over evil, and light over darkness. Yet the world is shot through with signs of your love and power. Give us eyes to see you at work, and faith to know that you will triumph and that we will share in your victory.

85 Church triumphant

John's next scene relies on the book of Daniel. Daniel saw thrones set up, and books opened (Daniel 7:9–10). He made no mention of who sat on the thrones, or what was in the books. John is a little less cryptic.

The figures on the thrones are almost certainly the martyrs whom he sees raised to life. Their souls have been waiting under the altar of the heavenly temple (6:9–11). Now their full number has been reached. The Church's task of witness is ended, and they enter into their reward. Clothed in their resurrection bodies, they share the rule of Christ and have a part in his judgment (Matthew 19:28; 1 Corinthians 6:2).

Outlasting the beast

The martyrs who share Christ's rule are not just those who have literally been beheaded. That is a figure of speech. Indeed, they are not only those who have literally been martyred, but are all the members of the Church which John characterizes as martyred. They are the faithful witnesses who have not been seduced or bullied into worshipping the beast.

This is the real point of the millennium. In this world, the beast appears triumphant. The true witnesses of Christ are judged by it and put to death. The power of the godless structures of the world seems irrefutable and irresistible. Yet in the final analysis, it is the beast which perishes in flames, and the martyred Church which rises triumphant.

We have already see this 'first resurrection' at 11:11. The martyred witnesses triumph over death, and through their life bring the nations to faith. Now the resurrection of the martyrs is shown as a part of Christ's rule and judgment on the beast and the nations.

The description of the martyrs in the millennium passage is entirely in terms which contrast them with the beast. The beleaguered Christians to whom John writes might well be tempted to wonder whether their resistance and witness were worthwhile. The temptation to compromise with the beast might seem even more appealing when set against the alternative of martyrdom. So the millennium passage exhorts them (and us!) to open their eyes to the reality of the rule they share with Christ, and assures them that this reality will not remain hidden forever. They are now priests of God, mediating his reality to the world (1:6; 5:10). This too, will be acknowledged by all when the end comes.

Now and not yet

The millennium therefore faces in two directions in time. It looks forward to the new creation, the final judgment and the resurrection of all the dead. At the same time the role of the Church remains what it is now: to share the rule of Christ, to be his priests and to affirm the truth of its testimony to Jesus.

To this extent, the 'Amillennial' view is right. The millennium, though set in the future, confirms the role of the martyr Church in living out, in the presence of the beast, the values of the coming kingdom. Through the death and resurrection of Jesus, and the witness of the Church, the kingdom has a foothold in the world. Those who share in the work of the kingdom here can be assured of a final glorious outcome.

Because of his stress on the call to witness, and to suffer as necessary for the truth of the gospel, John may seem to have little to say about any present blessings which Christians may experience. By stressing the coming and present share in Christ's reign, he points to the real strength of Christianity in the present age. To be a Christian is to know God, and to experience, in however limited a way, his presence, his love and the empowering of his Spirit. Against this, the beast has nothing to offer.

PRAYER
Father, thank you for your promised victory. Help your people in this world to see that they already have a share in it, and know your blessing now.

86 Eternal consequences

Once the thousand year reign of Christ is ended, Satan is set free, and the nations once again rebel. We need not ask where the nations come from if they have been destroyed at the end of chapter 19 (nor indeed, over whom the saints rule in the millennium, on the same count). This is the language of symbolism, borrowed from Ezekiel. In Ezekiel 37–40 John found a similar pattern, of resurrection, the restoration of God's people under the rule of the Messiah, invasion by the forces of Gog, and the coming of the new Jerusalem.

The point is that in this world, there will always be Satan, for he represents the human tendency to sin. There will always be 'the nations' for they represent the human tendency to set up systems and structures which oppose God. Nothing less than a new creation will see an end to this pattern, not even the direct rule of the earth by the risen Christ.

Dwelling of God

Once again the armies of evil surround the camp of the saints. The term, 'camp' brings us once again to the exodus theme which runs through Revelation. The people of God in this world are on a journey which will lead to the new Jerusalem. This has not yet come into being, so the 'beloved city' is a reference to the camp of God's people.

Wherever the Church is gathered, there is the dwelling of God, and there is the city of God. Like the tabernacle of the wilderness wanderings, the presence of God moves with his people as protector, teacher and guide. It may perhaps be hard to us to recognize the city of God in the midst of our world, and in the midst of our local congregation. But then, we rarely see things as God does.

Gog and Magog descend on the saints. In Ezekiel 38:2, Gog is king of the land of Magog. John makes them both either lands or kings. In both books, the names are simply symbols for the enemies of God.

Once again, there is no battle. Fire falls from heaven and destroys them.

Lake of fire

Satan is now finally destroyed, heralding the coming of the new age, the new creation. He is destined to an eternity of torment in the lake of fire with the beast and the false prophet.

This raises a rather important question, especially since they will shortly be joined by those human beings who have rejected God (14:10; 20:14–15). Does John truly envisage an eternity of suffering for those who are not saved?

To be sure, the Church has taught this for a long time (though never without dissent), but as far as Revelation is concerned there are good indicators that we are once again reading the language of symbol rather than fact. Firstly, the beast and the false prophet are abstractions, symbols themselves, as indeed are Death and Hades (20:13). It is impossible to speak of these being eternally tormented, though for sinners and the devil it may make more sense. Secondly, the lake of fire is described as the second death, which is the language of final ending. The eternal torment, like the smoke of fallen Babylon, which goes up forever (19:3) is better taken as a figure of speech, indicating the eternal and irrevocable consequences of rejecting God's offer of salvation.

A third point which we need to bear in mind in making doctrine, if not in reading Revelation, is philosophical. God is the creator and sustainer of all. To have an eternal hell of torment, with no remission nor hope of repentance, is to have God sustaining, in his perfect new creation, a part of it which will always be in rebellion against him, and which can only be described as evil. It would also make nonsense of the promise in 21:4 that there will be no more mourning, crying and pain. It would be sensible to go with those parts of the book which indicate a final ending, an annihilation, of those who are not redeemed.

PRAYER

Father, let the seriousness of rejecting you give urgency to our witness.

Book of life

After the interlude of millennium and rebellion comes the last judgment. God appears seated on a throne which is now the white of victory, and creation dissolves at his appearing. Both the earthly world and the spiritual dimension that lies behind it are stripped away. All that remains is God, and those he is to judge.

The disappearance of creation is not a great act of destruction like the fall of Babylon. It is simply a clearing of the site, ready for God's re-creation of the new heaven and earth. It has served its purpose. It has brought forth creatures who can know and love God, and so find an eternal destiny with him—or be lost forever.

Deeds and destiny

All the dead are raised for judgment, even those with no grave save the depth of the sea. But who are these dead? Presumably, they are all those who have not been raised already, for the millennial reign. In other words, they are those who did indeed follow the beast, who were not included in the number of the Church. We might expect their judgment to be superfluous. The books with their recorded deeds will show only evil. They will not be in the book of life, and so their fate is sealed.

However, things are not so simple. Verse 15 tells us that anyone whose name was not in the book of life was cast into the fire. The implication is that some were not, for their names were in the book. Moreover, the very fact that the books must be consulted suggests that there is something to be said in their favour.

Twice, John stresses that judgment is on the basis of their deeds, yet at the same time, it depends on the book of life. The implication is that their deeds reflect their status before God. Actions spring from faith—faith in God, or faith in something else. Can it be that there are those whose deeds are the deeds of faith in God, but who are somehow not counted as part of the martyred people of God? The answer would seem to be yes.

Open verdict

In the crucial section of Revelation, 11:1–13, we see the witness of the suffering Church resulting in the salvation of the majority of those who had followed the beast (11:13). In the image of the two harvests (14:14–20) we see two possible results of the world's judgment. It may lead either to salvation or to destruction. There is no attempt to bring together these two images. They are left side by side, for the task of the Church is not yet ended, and even the prophet John cannot tell us how it will be resolved.

From chapter 15 onwards, the descriptions of judgment on the beast and Babylon have had the grape harvest in view. God's vintage of wrath is trodden, and the consequences shown in detail. Now the picture is more ambiguous. We are told that judgment takes place. Some suffer the second death. But how many? Exactly who? We are not told. The thrust of Revelation as a whole forbids a belief that salvation is given without repentance and faith on the part of the saved. Yet John's ambiguity here is a way of saying that repentance and faith may belong to more than we suspect. We are not given the right, as yet, to judge any. All we may do is proclaim the gospel, joyfully welcoming those who respond visibly, and leaving the final decision to God.

Harvest of life

From now on, the first harvest, the gathering in to eternal life (14:14–16) governs the visions. Judgment is past, for good or ill, and a new creation is to begin.

PRAYER

Father, protect us from the temptation to pass the judgment that is reserved for you. Instead, show us such a vision of your love that we will desire nothing more than to share it with others.

New creation

Judgment gives way to the new world. This has been the goal all along. History and faith have been directed towards it. Now John sees it. Of course, like the rest of Revelation, the description which follows is symbolic. There can be no description of something which no one living has experienced. At the same time, there are hints of what it will be; hints found in worship and prayer, in the beauty and harmony of the present creation. Hints which are found in the present possibility of a relationship with God, for the centre of the new creation, like the centre of present reality (4:2–4) is God himself. Where he is presently hidden from sight, he will be in plain view.

Renewal

In his description of the new creation, John draws on the old. He does not envisage a total replacement, but a renewal (verse 5). What is to come is based on what already is, but it will be greater, purer and more fully itself.

So John sees a new heaven and a new earth. Heaven too must be renewed, since it stands for the spiritual reality of the present age. As such it had a place for the devil, who is no more. The sea too, is gone. For those who see the seas as the greatest beauty of the earth, this is at first a startling image. A new creation without the thunder of breakers, the rich diversity of the ocean deeps and the haunting cry of gulls seems strangely impoverished. It is not the physical sea of earth that is in view, however. The crystal sea before the throne of God has gone. It symbolized the forces of chaos, which have their spiritual as well as earthly counterparts. Towards the end of the book, it became the lake of fire (15:2), symbol of eternal destruction and separation from God. It stood for the Red Sea, a barrier to the people of God, and for the abyss out of which evil comes, and which must be overcome by the creative power of God. In the new creation, these are things of the past. The spiritual realm is purified, and it becomes the spring of harmony and peace.

Goal of creation

If this is the final destiny of creation, we might ask why God did not just create it straight away. It might have saved a lot of trouble, after all!

This is not a question John is concerned to answer, nor does it appear elsewhere in the Bible. The scriptures start where we are, in the here and now, and address what it means to know God in the real world, rather than in a fantasy realm. All the same, the question is a fair one, and the answer is in fact implied throughout the Bible, and especially in Revelation.

God's desire is for people who will freely love and serve him. In the world at large, there are certain values which he treasures, such as love, honesty, integrity, faithfulness, compassion and mercy. The processes by which such values may come about can only be found in a world such as ours. They need a world where there is the possibility of disobedience, so that obedience can be freely offered; where love is given against the potential for hatred; where service is a real alternative to selfishness. Only if sin is a real possibility can virtue be meaningful. Honesty, integrity and faithfulness demand the possibility of falsehood; compassion and mercy need cruelty and legalism as real options. God does not desire that any of these bad things actually happen, but they must be real possibilities. Only when love and virtue have been freely offered can they be preserved for eternity in the new creation. So Revelation is a call to the faithful witness to God's love and mercy which will one day be seen by all.

PRAYER

Lord, give us grace to use our freedom for you.

City of God

It has been said that Revelation could be subtitled, 'A Tale of Two Cities'. All that can be said of the two sides in the conflict between the purposes of God and of Satan are summed up in their representatives, Babylon and the New Jerusalem.

For the Christians of John's churches, as with most inhabitants of Greek and Roman society, life outside a city was unthinkable. Their identity was formed by the city in which they lived, by its culture, its social life, its local politics and its religion. This was what made the claims of Christianity so difficult for many believers. The call to disassociate themselves from much that their neighbours took for granted—the trade guilds, the social and religious life of the pagan temples, the enthusiastic support of the empire itself—led to a sense of being outsiders in their own home community.

The same can apply to Christians today. It is obvious in, for instance, an ardently Muslim country. Even in more 'liberal' Western nations, those who take their faith and witness seriously can feel that they have become to some extent outsiders in their workplace, their local pub or even their family.

So Christians looked for another city, which could give them their sense of belonging and identity. For John's readers, then and now, that city of God belongs to the future. In some sense, as we have seen, it is present wherever God is acknowledged and worshipped. The community of believers becomes itself the dwelling place of God (13:6). The only tangible city, however, tends to be Babylon and its satellites, the great whore who is the mother of whores (17:5), that is, the other cities of the empire, or of the world.

In the climactic visions of Revelation, John assures us that the time will come when the city of God, the new Jerusalem, will be a reality—the only reality.

City of hope

The fact that John's hope is couched in terms of a city should counteract one false impression that Revelation can give: that the city must always be a symbol of evil. In the ancient word, the city was the symbol of order and dignity, of art and culture. It was the city that enabled the flourishing of law and art, of philosophy and religion. It is a view that has passed into our language. Politics, police, policy and polite are a few of the words we draw from *polis*, the Greek word for city. The Latin word for city is *civitas*, from which our own word 'city' comes. It is also the source of our words citizen, civilization, civility and a host of others.

The vision of the new Jerusalem confirms this idea, that human beings are intended to live in communities where all that is good may flourish, where they may interact for their common good, and share love, understanding and faith. Without the city, much that we call civilization could not exist, and in the new creation all that is good in the city will be preserved for ever.

Witness

With the vision of new Jerusalem before it, the Church's witness must surely include working to make the cities of the present world reflect to some extent the world which is to come. We cannot wash our hands of the cities in which most of us live, for God has decreed that we will live in a city forever. Like the Jews who were exiled to Babylon, Christians must work for the good of their present city, bringing to it the values and faith of the city of God (Jeremiah 29:1–14). There will always be much of Babylon in our cities; but there can be something of Zion too.

PRAYER

Father, we bring before you the people who dwell in cities. May they discover a sense of community, of hope and of acceptance which reflects your eternal city.

90 Eternal love, eternal life

The new Jerusalem comes down from heaven, for it is the gift of God. The God to whom all history is moving, the God who is coming to meet his people, is a gracious God. He is the giver of eternal life, and the one who has prepared a place for his people.

The city of God is more than a place. It is the presence of God himself. He is the dwelling place of his people. His presence surrounds and protects, sustains and nourishes. He is the source of all true hope, all life, and all meaning. The words translated in NRSV as 'home' and 'dwell' (verse 3) are literally 'tent' or 'tabernacle' and its related verb. They call to mind once more the story of the exodus, as God dwelt among his people in the holy tent, and led them to the promised land. More than that, the Greek words used are the ones normally used to translate the Hebrew, *shekinah*, the glowing cloud which shows the presence of God's glory (Exodus 40:34; 1 Kings 8:10–11). That luminous glory is now to be among his peoples for ever (see Ezekiel 37:27–28; Zechariah 2:10–11).

The many peoples of God

The various early manuscripts of Revelation are divided as to whether God promises that those amongst whom he will dwell are to be his 'people', or his 'peoples'. Each is found in English versions, so that, for instance, RSV has 'people' and NRSV has 'peoples'. The plural is the best one to go for, since the weight of evidence favours it. It is also easier to see how a puzzled scribe might change it to the singular, so that it would refer to the single people of God, rather than the other way round.

This is an important point, because it shows the breadth of the vision of the city of God. It is the presence of God with all the peoples of the earth. Once again we are brought to the hopeful vision of the grain harvest of chapter 14. John's picture of eternal life includes the vast numbers who have responded to the witness of the suffering Church, and have been brought into the everlasting kingdom of God. If the vision of the world to come is meant as an inspiration to the Church, it is a vision which includes the salvation of the majority, rather than a select few. We are called to witness in this hope, not in a sense of pessimism or despair. It is also important to note that there is no distinction here between those who have suffered and died for their faith, and the greater host of peoples who enter because of their witness. All are God's peoples, whether they come early or late to receive his grace (Matthew 20:1–16).

Loving God

Three times we are told that God will be with his peoples, and in words of tender intimacy (borrowed from Isaiah 25:8) told that he will wipe away every tear from their eyes. It is the image of a caring parent, bringing comfort to a bruised child. It is also a picture of direct action. This is something God will do. It will not be delegated to angels, to saints, or even to Jesus himself. There are no barriers or intermediaries, but only the living presence of the loving God himself.

John uses the word, 'love', very little. It is significant that the book as a whole is bracketed with images of love. It begins with an assertion that salvation springs from God's love (1:5) and ends with the personal presence of that love.

This is a love which banishes death itself, and spells the end to all its associated misery. The first world, in which we now live, is a necessary prelude to the new creation. But it is a prelude only. The eternal love is the eternal reality.

PRAYER

Father, as history is bracketed by your love, may it also be the beginning and ending of our lives, and the one characteristic which marks us as yours.

91

Goal of creation

At various points in Revelation, a voice has been heard from the throne. The context has sometimes suggested that the speaker is God. Now, for the first time, it is clearly stated that God speaks. The direct speech, neither mediated by an angel, nor coming as a distant voice, is another indication of God's dwelling with his people.

He is making all things new. The idea is of renewal rather than simple replacement. Creation is God's handiwork, and so is valuable and worthy of preservation. The new creation is a fulfilment of the old, rather than a simple replacement of it. Paul, writing to the Romans, saw the whole of creation as being involved in God's plan of salvation. All that God has made awaits a final transformation (Romans 8:22).

Message of hope

The news that a new creation awaits, that there is hope and purpose for the world, is worth sharing. John is told to write it down, so that it can be spread to many. Christianity is not a mystery religion, whose teaching is accessible only to those who have been initiated. It is not a form of Gnosticism, where salvation comes through arcane teachings. There have been times in the Church's history when both these mistakes have been made. They have usually been condemned as heresy, though occasionally the official attitude of the Church has been to keep the deep teachings of the faith restricted to a chosen few. By ordering that it be written down (and read aloud—1:3), God himself declares that his word is for everyone.

It is a message to be shared, a vision to be spread abroad, so that all may hear, and receive God's gift of salvation. It is a message to be trusted, as it comes from the one who is himself steadfast and trustworthy.

In his vision, John hears the fulfilment of the promise. God declares his purposes to be complete. Creation has reached its final point, and achieved what God has desired. He has a people—many diverse peoples—who acknowledge him freely, who offer their worship and service as loving children, and receive his own eternal love and blessing.

Precious creation

We cannot begin to understand the form that the new creation will take, any more than we can imagine what life will be like after resurrection. The nearest we can come is imagery and analogy (e.g. 1 Corinthians 15:35–44). We have the promise, and that must be enough. At the same time, the fact that the promise of renewal is for all creation has a definite significance for the present. It reinforces the biblical doctrine that human beings are a part of the whole of creation.

That may sound so obvious as to be trite. Yet the way we use our world, destroying resources, plant and animal species, polluting air and seas, suggests that we see it as a thing apart from our selves. It is approached as something which we can manipulate and use for our own ends, without consequences for us.

This is not so. There is certainly something unique about human beings. They have the capacity for moral action, and the ability to relate to God. In the Genesis stories of creation, this uniqueness is described as being in the image of God (Genesis 1:27) and being animated by his spirit, or breath (Genesis 2:7). At the same time, humans are called into being by the same creative command of God as all other things (Genesis 1) and are formed from the same earth as all other animals (Genesis 2:7).

We are made to be part of a universe which affects us as we affect it, and on which our lives depend. We damage ourselves when we do it harm. For this same reason, we are destined forever to be part of a greater creation. Our ultimate destiny is connected with that of the world, and vice versa.

PRAYER

Thank you, God, that we are part of a greater whole. Instil in us a respect and a sense of wonder for all your works.

92
Beginning and end

All this is the work of the God who is the beginning and the end of creation. He has made it and he will bring it to fruition. The description of God as beginning and end, Alpha and Omega, is more than a statement of the origin and destiny of the universe. By encompassing the start and the finish, it describes in shorthand the biblical doctrine of God as sustainer and guide of all that he has made.

The Bible has no concept of a God who winds up the universe like clockwork, and then leaves it to run along on its own. God is intimately involved in his works, a part of the system he has made, and the motive force behind it.

To say this does not imply that we have to accept a fundamentalist view of creation, and say that the biblical stories of origins are literally true. It does say that all the complex processes of evolution and development, from the formation of stars and galaxies to the appearance of life on earth, are purposeful, and guided by God.

Chance and purpose

There is a fashionable strand of thought which claims that the discoveries of scientists working on the origins of the universe, or on the processes of evolution, have left no place for belief in a God who is the creator. Even less place, it is claimed, is left for the notion of purpose in a mechanism that depends on random events.

A popular commentary on Revelation is not the place to argue against such views in detail, but no modern discussion of creation can afford to ignore them. Suffice it to say that there is a vast difference between what science actually says, and what some of its interpreters claim for it. We can say that modern research suggests a process of development, and a mechanism by which it (at least in part) comes about. What we cannot say is that these mechanisms are purposeless. The only world where we have studied the development of life suggests very strongly that it is oriented to the production of complex, conscious, moral and spiritual beings.

We may choose to see the world as a vast battle ground in which the fittest survive and the rest go to the wall; an amoral jungle of competing species and individuals. In such a world, it is hard indeed to see the hand of God. But we may choose instead to see the world as a vast and complex system of interlocking relationships, engaged in the quest for greater and more wonderful forms of life, and which brings forth the beings God desires. On such a view, the reality of death and decay is a necessary part of the process which continually refines and develops the world. In such a world, there is every evidence of a sustaining and directing creator.

Life-giver

It is this God, creator, sustainer and saviour, who gives the promise of eternal life. It is he who is able to satisfy the soul-thirst that leaves us seeking more in the presence of plenty, and which declares that there must be hope in the face of despair, and meaning when all seems pointless. In him alone is true satisfaction found.

In the new creation, the living water promised by Jesus (John 4:10; 7:37–38), and which is fulfilled in part through the gift of the Holy Spirit, becomes an eternal reality.

PRAYER

Lord, you have made us for yourself, and our
souls are restless till they find their rest in you.
St Augustine

Children of God

The messages to the seven churches each ended with a promise to the one who conquers. We have seen what it means to conquer. It is to be faithful in witness even to the point of death. The promises referred forward to the last two chapters of the book, and now that is made explicit. It is the wonders of the new creation, the new Jerusalem, which lie in wait for those who remain faithful to Christ.

By now it should be clear that this promise is not 'pie in the sky when you die'. The vision of the world to come is a driving force behind the Church's present witness and worship. It is foreshadowed in the present experience of the Spirit of God, and tasted in the believer's relationship with Christ. Above all it is presaged by the present privilege of being called God's children.

Children were one of Jesus' favourite images for his disciples (Matthew 7:11; 18:2-5, 6; 19:14; John 13:33; 21:5). It was an image of trust and dependence. Children rely on their parents for their very lives, and so Jesus' disciples were to rely on God. Even more than this, it was an image of love and acceptance. The followers of Jesus are servants of God, his slaves (Romans 1:1; Revelation 1:1, and so on). They are ambassadors of God (2 Corinthians 5:20) and his stewards (1 Corinthians 4:1). All of these can be positions of responsibility and privilege. They can also be positions of fear and unease. But to be children of God is to be welcomed into the family circle, to know love and peace, safety and well-being. As a valued child, even rebuke and punishment are given with love in mind, and proper growth as the goal (1 Corinthians 4:14). In the new creation, the goal has been achieved, and there remains only the eternal welcome home.

Cast out

It comes as something of a shock suddenly to be confronted with a reminder of those who are not to share in the new order. Surely judgment is now past, and only glory remains? True enough, as the order of John's story goes. It is written, though, as an encouragement and challenge to the churches. The promise has been given to the conquerors, but a warning is given to those who are tempted to compromise with the world.

The first on the list of Christians who may be in danger of failure are cowards; those who are put off from the life of faithful witness by fear, and so prove faithless to Jesus. We might expect some mention of the loveless and the hypocrites, those who were most roundly condemned by Jesus himself. Not to mention the nagging thought that courage is not a virtue that most people would claim with any certainty! John, however, is writing from a particular viewpoint. He wants to call his churches to be witnesses who will remain true to their Lord in the face of the persecuting beast. In times of strong opposition, courage is the cardinal virtue. Fortunately it is also a gift of God. It is there for those who would be faithful.

The rest of the list reflects the charges brought against the whore Babylon and the beast on which she rode. To compromise with the forces of the world, is to be identified with the sins of the world. Few members of John's churches are likely to have been murderers or sorcerers, but if they tried to steer a quiet middle path of compromise, they were tacitly siding with the power which kills the saints of God, and claims an authority which is his alone.

Some interpreters argue that this passage must be about unbelievers, since no Christian can truly be lost. In the present context, it must refer to members of the churches, for only they have been called to conquer, and the very call itself presupposes the possibility of refusal.

PRAYER

Father, in your love you have called us to be your children. Help us to rely on you for the courage we sometimes need as members of your family.

Beloved bride

The theme of warning to the churches continues in the appearance of one of the seven bowl angels. It is the instrument of God's wrath who invites the prophet to have a closer look at the city of God. The presence of the judging angel points up the choice which faces the Church, and through the Church's witness, the nations of the world. They may belong to Babylon or to the city of God. In less symbolic terms, they may, by their choice of god (the beast or the true God) make their own dwelling resemble either Babylon or new Jerusalem.

Intimate love

We have seen the city of God represented as a place in which the peoples will dwell. In that sense, it stands for God's new creation, the remade universe which will be the environment for the redeemed. We have also seen it shown as the presence of God himself. His being and love will surround and sustain his creation. Of course, it already does, but the spiritual reality which underlies all things will be a tangible experience in the age to come. Now we are shown the city as people, the redeemed of God.

This has been hinted at already in the promise that the victors will be God's children (verse 7). Now another image of intimate love is brought into play. The city of God, whose beauty is like that of a bride in all her finery (verse 2) turns out in fact to *be* the bride, the one who is married to the Lamb.

The image of God's people as his wife has a long history in the Bible. Hosea had likened the love of God to his own experience with a faithless wife. They had turned away and worshipped other gods, just as Hosea's wife, Gomer, had been a prostitute in the Canaanite fertility cults (Hosea 1–3). God would none the less bring his people back to himself; a process which would be painful to both God and Israel. Now the new Jerusalem appears as the bride of the Lamb— the one who has brought them back to God at great personal cost. The reconciliation has been achieved through the shedding of blood: the blood of Christ, and the blood of the martyrs.

The picture of God's search for his faithless wife led to the image of a relationship of intimacy and love between God and his people which is as deep and passionate as any sexual relationship. Jews and Christians came to read the Bible's great love poem, the Song of Songs, as an allegory of the love of God for his people. It was read particularly at Passover, the festival of God's rescue of his people. The same image is used of the relationship of Christ to the Church (Ephesians 5:28–32).

Divine longing

Such an image does much to dispel the notion of God as a distant and probably angry figure of power. It is the language of passion, of a longing which is as intense as pain. God is no calculating cosmic architect. He is the father who sees his children on the path to ruin, the lover whose bride has left him at the altar to seek a road to self-destruction. It is this divine pain which finds expression on the cross, and shows itself as redeeming love. It is this heartfelt desire for the good and the love of his creatures which lies behind the language of jealousy which characterizes God in the Old Testament (Exodus 20:5).

This rich tradition is now applied to Jesus and the people he has redeemed. Once again, he is worthy to be addressed in terms befitting God, for he is indeed God, come to be one of us. To woo his bride, God has become a human being and suffered human pain.

PRAYER

Eternal God, we cannot measure the depth of your love. We can only wonder at its immensity and lose ourselves within it.

95

Meeting place

By now we should not be surprised to find John describing once again something he has already shown us. It has been the pattern of much of his book. He now looks in more detail at the holy city, and explains its significance.

Spirit of prophecy

Once again, the Spirit of God whisks him away on a visionary trip. The footnote in NRSV ('in the Spirit') is a better translation than the main text's 'in the spirit'. This is not something which happens in John's spirit, but is the work of the Holy Spirit. The phrase 'in the Spirit' occurs four times at significant points in the book. It introduces the whole work as a visionary experience which brought the words of Christ to him (1:10) and begins the series of visions of heaven and the reality which underlies the world (4:2). It is the Spirit who opens his eyes to the spiritual significance of Rome (17:3) and now shows him the meaning of the new Jerusalem, the city which is the pattern of all true cities, and of which Babylon is a poisonous travesty.

The Spirit is not the one who speaks and gives the revelation. That is a chain of communication which leads from God, through Christ to the angel of chapter 10 (1:1). The work of the Spirit, as the inspirer of prophecy, is to grant John the visionary experiences through which such communication becomes possible. This is a view of the Spirit's work which we find elsewhere in the New Testament. The Spirit is the one who makes Christ real to us, so that we can hear him speak, the one who opens up a relationship with God which makes worship possible (Romans 8:15; Galatians 4:6), who forms a channel for our prayer (Romans 8:26–27) and who carries the revelation of God himself (1 Corinthians 2:10–12).

These four references to the Spirit's visionary inspiration may perhaps point to the original visions on which John has reflected and prayed to produce his book. (The finished work, of course, is a piece of carefully written theological literature.)

Mountain of God

The mountain to which John is carried is not merely a vantage point from which he can get a better view. It is the mountain to which the city itself descends (Ezekiel 40:2), and it is full of symbolism. In primitive thought, mountains are likely to be holy places, since they are nearer to the gods. The gods of Greek myth dwelt on Mount Olympus, and closer to biblical home, the Canaanite gods dwelt on a mythical mountain to the far north. This myth is hijacked by the writer of Psalm 48 and applied to Zion, the mountain of Jerusalem where the true God dwells in his temple (Psalm 48:1–2). It was at Mount Sinai that God revealed himself to the Israelites (Exodus 19:9–18). It was to Sinai (also called Horeb) that Elijah fled to meet with God (1 Kings 19:8) after showing the supremacy of YHWH over the gods of Canaan on Mount Carmel (1 Kings 18:20–40).

The high mountain of new Jerusalem signifies once again the meeting of God and his people. It is the place where God is encountered, the final reality of God's dwelling with his people.

In the present age this is a spiritual truth. God is with his people, and they are securely kept by the Lamb on his holy mount (14:1). In our worship and prayer we can meet consciously with God, and sometimes catch a glimpse of his reality. In the age to come, there is no distinction between spiritual and physical. There is one reality, apprehended by those who are called to spend eternity in the presence of God, whose reality suffuses the new creation.

PRAYER

Lord, thank you for those moments when your Spirit grants us a vision of your constant presence. May we always be aware of you, until the time when we meet you in your new creation.

96

Shining city

The detailed description of the holy city combines the themes we have noted so far. It shines with the glory of God, the glowing cloud of the *shekinah* which showed God's presence in the temple of old. It is translucent, so that the glory may shine from it, and its appearance is like jasper—the precious stone to which God himself is compared (4:3). Once again, the dwelling of the saints is seen as the presence of God.

Priests of the king

The walls are adorned with jewels, but these are no random selection of trinkets. They are the jewels found in the breastplate of the high priest (Exodus 28:17–20). (There is a slight difference between John's list and that of Exodus, but it is hard to be sure exactly what the names of precious stones in Hebrew refer to, and they had no fixed Greek equivalents.) Like the high priest's breastplate, the city is square, the geometric shape symbolizing perfection, and bears twelve jewels. In fact the city is a perfect cube, symbolizing its absolute perfection (perfection squared!). The city therefore has a priestly function, since it is also the people of God, his royal priesthood.

In the new creation, there is no need for a priesthood to mediate the presence of God to the nations. The witnessing task of the Church is ended. The other task of a priesthood, that of offering worship, goes on eternally. The city symbolizes the worshipping community of the redeemed.

Eternal worship

A brief warning may be in order at this point. We must not think of the life of the new creation as one of an eternal church service! No matter how enjoyable our worship may be, the thought of doing it forever without a break makes the age to come thoroughly unattractive. To speak of the new creation as eternal worship is to speak of an eternal awareness of the presence and glory of God, rather than an endless liturgy or prayer meeting or whatever.

Paradise regained

The city is also the place which God has prepared for his people to live in. It symbolizes the whole of the new creation as the habitat of the redeemed peoples. In this sense, it is paradise restored. According to Jewish interpretation, Havilah, the land adjacent to Eden (Genesis 2:11–12) was counted as part of Paradise. It was there that gold and precious stones were to be found in abundance. The New Jerusalem is built out of the materials of Eden, and so is a return to the glory God originally intended for his creatures. The angels at the gates are a further indication that the holy city is a kind of return to Paradise. When God cast Adam and Eve out of the garden, he set the cherubim (an order of angels) to guard the way back (Genesis 3:24). Now the angels stand at the gates to open them in welcome.

Better than Paradise

The city, while it reflects the restoration of the glory lost at the Fall, is not Eden remade. The garden which humanity was to till has been replaced by the community centred on God. Even God cannot undo what has been done. Innocence has been lost and cannot be restored. The way is not back, but forward, through the consequences of sin, the cross, resurrection and judgment, into a creation which takes account of all that has happened, and by the grace of God transforms the world's pain into the world's joy.

PRAYER

Father, thank you that you can take the greatest disaster, and re-create it to your glory, and our salvation.

97 The never-ending story

The gates of the city bear the names of the twelve tribes of Israel. The last time we heard of the tribes, they stood for the Church (7:4–8). This time, they stand for historic Israel.

This becomes clear when we see that the foundations of the city are inscribed with the names of the twelve apostles. The city, then, represents the whole people of God. It is founded on the apostles, and entry into it is into the covenant people of God.

The new Jerusalem is the culmination of a process which has its origins in the call of Abraham, the rescue of the Israelites from Egypt and the forging of God's people in the desert of Sinai. Indeed, it goes back further, to the first human choice of sin, lost in the mists of pre-history, and shrouded in the Hebrew myths of Eden and the serpent. It was the goal of the people of God, symbolized but never realized in historic Jerusalem, the temple, and the dream of Messiah.

It was made possible by the coming of Christ, and is partially realized in the worship and witness of his people. It is the promise and goal of his Church.

The story of the people of God is the story of the outworking of his salvation. It is a story of which we are as much a part as any character in the Bible. The call to witness which forms the backbone of Revelation is a call to all Christians to take their place in the story which leads from Eden to the new Jerusalem.

Heavenly surveyor

Once before, we have seen measurements being taken. John was told to measure the temple of God (11:1) as a sign of God's protection of his people. On that occasion, the outer court was left unprotected; God's people would be trampled underfoot, though their relationship with God was safe.

All is measured because suffering is at an end. There are no more foes to conquer the outward aspect of the people. The victory has been won and God's peace rules over his people.

The measuring angel finds the dimensions of the city to be multiples of twelve, the number of the people of God. It is a cube, sign of perfection, and also the shape of the Holy of Holies, the innermost sanctuary of the earthly temple built by Solomon (1 Kings 6:20). It was in there that the presence of God dwelt. The city is found to represent the people of God, and to be his dwelling place.

Temple city

There is no temple in the city, for the whole of it is filled with the glory of God. There is no central place of worship, for all the inhabitants are priests who see God face to face (22:4), and the character of their very existence is worship and service.

A similar thought lies behind the wall of jasper. It is built of the stone which represents God. Zechariah had prophesied that in the restored Jerusalem, God himself would be its wall of fire (Zechariah 2:5). No wall is really necessary, but the presence of a wall was what defined a city in John's day. The city of God is defined by his presence. He is its eternal security.

Living in the midst of the divine glory (which comes from both God and the Lamb) there is no need of external illumination. The sun and moon are rendered redundant by the light of God himself (Isaiah 60:19–20—Isaiah 60 lies behind verses 23–26).

PRAYER

Lord, help us too see our role in your story, and your will for our lives, until the day we see you face to face.

98 Saviour of the nations

The city of God lies open to the nations of the world and their kings. These are the ones who trampled the outer court of the temple (11:2) in their persecution of the Church, who were seduced by the whore (17:2; 18:3, 23), and who were destroyed in their final rebellion by the returning Christ (19:15). In the present scenario, they have repented and entered into the promised salvation (11:13; 15:4). John's picture of the new creation builds on the possibility held out by the harvest of grain (14:14–16). He does not set before us a corresponding image of a city peopled only by the martyrs.

If John does not explicitly choose between the two possibilities, his final vision is the optimistic one. Human beings are free to reject even the love of God, but they do so in the face of the faithful proclamation of the gospel. John knew that the word of God does not go out in vain (Isaiah 55:9–11).

Redeemed creation

The nations and their kings bring their glory and honour into the city. These terms can also be translated as treasure and wealth, and that is how they should be understood. In Isaiah's vision of the restored Jerusalem, the kings come in homage to Zion, bringing offerings of all the treasures of the earth (Isaiah 60:8–12).

Unlike Isaiah's vision, they do not come to the new Jerusalem as servants of the saints, but as equal sharers in its glory. What they bring is all that is good in the earth. Only those things which are unacceptable to God are excluded.

Those who once brought their goods to adorn the whore now bring them into the city of God. The new creation is not a place of austerity, but of richness and splendour. Nothing that is good in the present age will be lost, but it will be transformed into greater wonder.

The Bible does not present us with a world-denying form of spirituality. It begins with the assertion that what God has made, he pronounced good (Genesis 1). If the world lay under his curse through human sin (Genesis 3:17; Romans 8:20–22), it was through no failing in creation. There is much that is good in the world, and it is the gift of God. In the new creation, the curse is removed, and the goodness remains.

At times, Christians have embraced a very negative view of the material world, scorning earthly pleasure as sinful, and earthly riches as wicked. John does not share this view. The wickedness of Babylon did not lie in the existence of wealth and splendour, but in the use to which it was put, and the human cost at which it was obtained.

Salvation is not a freeing of the soul from material being, but a transformation of the material into an eternal form. This is why the distinctively Christian view of 'life after death' is resurrection, not simply survival of the soul. God's salvation is universal and embraces all creation.

Warning

As in verse 8, John adds a salutary reminder. Nothing can enter the city which is opposed to God. That goes for the people of his churches too. There is no place for falsehood or that which corrupts.

PRAYER

Father, open our eyes to the goodness of your creation, and inspire us to use it well.

REVELATION 22:1–5
Water of life

The theme of Paradise restored continues with the river of life which runs through the streets of the city, and is bounded by the tree of life. the image is hard to imagine visually, but its message is clear. Jesus had promised eternal life, the life of the Spirit, as refreshing water (John 4:14; 7:38). In turn, he drew on the Old Testament images which inspire Revelation. Ezekiel had pictured a river flowing from the temple of restored Jerusalem, and bringing life to the land. There is no temple in the new Jerusalem, but the river still symbolizes the same thing. Life flows from the presence of God. Where he is, the world bursts into flower and fruit. Beside Ezekiel's river stood trees which bore fruit all year (Ezekiel 47:1–12; cf. Zechariah 14:8). For John, the trees are the tree of life (Genesis 2:9) which was denied to humanity by sin (Genesis 3:22). Now all may eat of it, all may be refreshed by the waters of eternity.

Eco-city

If the city of God is the ideal city, it is worth noting that it does not form a bastion against the encroachment of nature. Its central features are a river and a tree. The human struggle against unrestrained nature is seen by the Bible as a result of sin (Genesis 3:17). In the new creation, civilization and the natural world flow in harmony. Even in our world, a city with no parks and trees is a bare and arid place.

One to one

The most staggering feature of the city, though, is that the people will see God's face. In the biblical tradition to look on the face of God was more than human life could bear (Exodus 33:20–23). In the new creation, there will be no barrier of fear between God and his creatures. In their worship, they will gaze on his reality.

The people bear the name of God on their foreheads. They have already been marked as his (7:3), though here the thought may refer to the high priest's headpiece which was said in later Jewish sources to bear the name of God, YHWH. The priestly function of the people of God continues in the age to come, as worship is offered to God and to the Lamb.

As his servants, the people of the city share in the reign of God. This does not mean that there are some other people who are ruled. The martyrs and the nations and their kings have all entered the city, and all are now God's. To say that they share his reign is a way of saying that they share his glory, and dwell within it.

Eternal journey

John has now exhausted his store of Old Testament images, and brought his description of the age to come to a triumphant conclusion. It is not the end of the story. In fact, it is the beginning of the tale, but it is one which cannot be comprehended by those who are not yet in the new city. The journey of the Church and the nations moves towards the climax which John foretells. After that, who can say? Perhaps the journey continues, in an ever deeper exploration of God, his love and his new creation. The infinite God can never be exhausted, and his wonders can never come to an end. There will always be more to be discovered, and more service, worship and love to encounter.

John's vision is no more than the title page of the second volume in the story of creation and redemption. For those of us who are still in the first part, it is enough to know that there is a sequel, and that it is even better than the first.

PRAYER

Father, thank you for your promise of eternity. May we journey in faith, hope and love until we know even as we are known.

True prophet?

Although John does not describe himself as a prophet, he announces his book as prophecy, he describes his calling to prophesy, and he is described as one of the brotherhood of prophets (22:9). Perhaps he avoided the word because he was in conflict with others, such as 'Jezebel' of Thyatira (2:20) who were ready to claim the title while delivering false teaching.

But was John right? It is easy to say that one's words are prophecy, but how does the hearer know? The angel asserts that the words of God delivered by John are trustworthy and true. God's words always are, or he would not be God. But are the words those of God? There would be many who would want to argue with John's views on compromise with Roman culture and religion. John's assertion that blessing follows the readers and doers of his teaching (1:3; 22:7, 9), that cursing will fall on its detractors (22:18–19), that he has received it as divine revelation (1:1; 22:8) and that it is the word of God is no answer. It does, however, make a strong claim. If this really is prophecy, the word of God to his Church, then it is an important one.

Testing the spirits

In the early Church, prophets played an important role, both in leadership and teaching. This meant that an equally important emphasis was placed on the testing of prophecies (1 Corinthians 14:29; 1 John 4:1). It is hard to be sure exactly what criteria were used, but the main one was surely how well the prophecy conformed to the teaching of scripture (Deuteronomy 13:1–3). John goes out of his way to demonstrate that his prophecy is not only in line with scripture, but ties the prophecies of the Old Testament together.

From our point of view, the answer has already been given, since the Church as a whole has agreed that Revelation has a place in holy scripture. That place did not come easily, and there was a lot of debate before it was accepted, but accepted it was.

Even that, though, does not solve the issue completely. We still have to ask whether this portion of the Bible is prophecy, the word of God, to us. For instance, Leviticus, with its detailed laws relating to the Jewish temple's sacrificial worship, is scripture, but much of it cannot address Christians (or even modern Jews) directly, however useful it may be as a testimony to God's working in the past. Is Revelation a book of the past, or is it still speaking to us?

The answer will depend on whether it challenges us to follow Christ, to witness to him and stay loyal to him come what may. It will depend on whether it challenges us to worship God, Father, Son and Holy Spirit, and to worship him alone. It will depend on whether it sets before us a vision of heaven, of the new creation, which inspires us, draws us to it, and provokes our worship.

From the point of view of the present writer, it does all this and more. It challenges our assumptions about the role of the Church, the acceptability of modern culture, society and politics. For those of us who worship with a written liturgy, Revelation is the source of many of the praises we sing to God week by week.

Of course, it has shortcomings. It paints a simple black and white picture of the people of God versus the world, when the reality can be much more complex (though to be fair it hints also at the complexity). It can be misused, promoting fanaticism and bigotry. But at its best, it is a fitting climax to the canon (the accepted list) of scripture. It is indeed a message from the God who sets the spirits of prophets on fire with his word.

PRAYER

Father, set our spirits on fire with your Spirit of prophecy, that we too may speak your words of inspiration to you in worship, to each other in encouragement and to the world in witness.

Coming soon?

A voice breaks into the angel's speech—that of Jesus, affirming that his appearance is at hand. It is clear that John saw the coming persecution of the Church as a sign of the imminent return of Christ. His letter to the seven churches was written in a spirit of urgency which we find very difficult to understand. After nearly two thousand years, it is hard to feel the force of an approaching judgment. Of course, we can affirm that no one knows the day or the hour. It could come tomorrow. But there have been a lot of tomorrows since John wrote.

This difficulty was felt even during the New Testament period (2 Peter 3:3–4). We have to accept that it is nowadays impossible to feel the same emotional urgency as many of the first Christians did, and which we find reflected in the New Testament. One answer is to try to whip up such a sense of expectation by interpreting Revelation as a prediction of our own times. Unfortunately, this is not what Revelation is about, and throughout history those who have taken such an approach have been disappointed.

A better answer is to realize that what really counts, in Revelation and the rest of the New Testament, is not when these things will happen, but how Christians are to live, worship and witness before they come about. John's message, for all that it is written in the light of the imminent return of Christ, is mainly concerned with how the Church is to behave before then. Blessed (now) is the one who keeps (now) the words of the prophecy in this book. That should be our concern as well.

True worship

As once before (19:10) John gives way to the temptation to fall in homage at the feet of the great angel who has opened his visionary eyes. He is rebuked in the same terms as before. The angel is a creature, made, like human beings, to serve God. The very term, 'angel' simply means messenger, and as such the purpose of the angel is like that of the prophets. He is there to bring God's message. The only true object of worship is God.

In John's world, it might not have seemed strange, at least outside of Christian and Jewish circles, to offer worship to an angel. Pagan thought was happy with the notion of many beings who were in various degrees divine. For Jews and Christians, divinity was absolute, and belonged only to God (with whom Christians also identified Jesus). John's mistake still stands as a warning to any who are tempted to place that which is not God at the centre of their lives.

Open book

Most apocalypses were written in the name of a famous person of long ago, and were presented as though they were prophecies by that person. A good example of this is Daniel, written to give heart to the Jews who resisted the rule of Antiochus IV of Syria in the second century BC. So Daniel ends with the command to seal up the book (supposedly written during the Babylonian exile) until it will be needed (Daniel 12:9). John writes under his own name, for his contemporaries, and the book is to remain unsealed, its contents open to all.

It is not a book of secret wisdom for the chosen few, nor a book for a distant time, but a book of encouragement and challenge for the churches of the present; a book for the Church in all ages. It is a book for good and bad, pure and impure, at all times as they go about their daily lives. To the righteous it is a book of promise and hope, to the evil-doer it is a warning of judgment and a call to repentance. To both it is a call to be prepared (Matthew 24:37–39).

PRAYER

Lord, give us a desire to know you and to serve you, not at some time in the future, but now.

Yours faithfully

John's visions reached their climax in verse 5. Then, as it were, he was left standing with the angel, who assured him of the truth of the visions and their message. Into this broke the voice of Jesus, promising his coming. Now Jesus speaks again. He is coming to bring his reward to those who have done the work of God.

Once again, we need to stress that the language of reward and works goes together with the language of faith. These are the works which stem from faith in God. For the Church, they are the work of faithful witness, in all its far-reaching meaning. Those who have stood firm against the beast, who have spoken the words of the gospel boldly, who have lived out the values of new Jerusalem in the midst of Babylon will receive their reward. Christ is coming to pronounce to his faithful servants that they have done well.

Lord and God

Jesus' promise is trustworthy, as the words of God are trustworthy (verse 6), for Jesus is God. The promise is bolstered by Revelation's clearest statement of the divinity of Christ. Earlier, God has been described as the Alpha and the Omega, the beginning and the end (1:8; 21:6). Jesus has been called the first and the last; the same sense, but different words (1:17). Now all three titles are claimed by Christ. He is the Alpha and the Omega, the first and the last, the beginning and the end. It is from him, as from God, that all things come. He is the creative principle of God, which brought the universe into being (John 1:1–5). He is the goal of creation, which finds its meaning and fulfilment in him. He is the one who is coming to bring salvation to the world. John, who had been tempted to fall in worship before the angel, now hears the words of the one who truly is worthy of worship, for he and all creation was created to give glory to the one who now speaks.

Final greetings

Revelation is a book in the form of a letter. It is a letter from John, but it is even more a letter from Jesus. Verses 14–18 formally end the letter, and it is signed with the first-century equivalent of 'yours faithfully, Jesus'.

Like most of the New Testament letters, there is a closing exhortation to live out the Christian life. Here it takes the form of a repetition of the basic warning of the book. For those who are faithful, if need be, to the point of death, and wash their robes in the blood of martyrdom, which is the blood of the Lamb, there is life. For those who reject the offer of salvation there is nothing. They are outside the city, which is the new creation, and being outside they are separated from the source of life itself.

'Dogs' was a Jewish term of abuse for Gentiles, signifying that which is unclean, for dogs are among the unclean animals in Jewish Law (Matthew 7:6; 15:26). Here it may refer to the 'false Jews' who instigate persecution against Christians (Philippians 3:2–3). It is probably fair, though, to see a deeper meaning. Those who seek their salvation, their personal fulfilment, in self-gratification, in the abuse of power and the pursuit of illusion, become less than truly human. Humanity is created to find itself in God, and only in him can ultimate fulfilment be found.

PRAYER

Lord Jesus Christ, as we gaze on you in worship and adoration, may we see ourselves—the image of true humanity and the fulfilment of your creation.

103

Come, desire of nations

John, who has been the recipient of the visions and the messages has now disappeared from his own book. The last word belongs to Jesus who has sent his angel (via John) to the seven churches (in Greek, the 'you' is plural in verse 16) with a message for all the churches.

John shows by example what it is to proclaim the gospel. The message is about Jesus, not about the speaker. Those gifted with fine oratory or other means of witnessing need to remember that they are drawing attention to Jesus, not to themselves. Those who feel that their speech is poor, their deeds unworthy, can draw encouragement from the fact that it is Jesus, not they, who is the attraction of Christianity.

Promised one

Jesus is the one promised by scripture, the king of David's line (Isaiah 11:1), the glorious ruler from Israel (Numbers 24:17). He is the one whom the Church desires as a bride looks forward to her wedding. He is the one to whom the Holy Spirit, inspirer of worship and prayer, points his Church. His coming is the consummation of human hopes and desires, a release from longing and spiritual thirst, the realization of eternal life.

That eternal life is not just a future event. It is a present experience for those who come to him. Eternal life is not just a quantity, an endless existence. It is a quality, a richness of life, an exuberant overflowing of life which comes from knowing God and being joined to him through Christ (John 17:3; 10:10). So the call of the Church for Christ's future coming is coupled with his invitation to the thirsty to come now for satisfaction.

Sacred book

It is because the offer is so wonderful that the warning to those who adulterate it is so terrible. If the book is accepted as true prophecy, then there can be no watering down either of its promises or its warnings. There is a strong temptation to feel that the gospel should be 'nice'. The gospel is a two-edged sword. It brings the good news of God's stupendous love, and the terrible news of human sinfulness. It shows a God whose love reaches beyond human imagining, and yet is still all too resistible by human beings. Such resistance is self-destruction, and that too is part of the gospel. Let the message stand, says the prophet, and let people make their choice—of life or death.

Make it so

The final word is Christ's and it is a word of encouragement. He is coming. There is hope for a beleaguered Church, and for weary witnesses. In the darkest moments of life and faith, there is light on the horizon which shines from the city of God. It is the destination of the saints and the goal of all true human aspirations. He will triumph, and all things will be well, and all manner of things will be well.

What can we say to that? Only amen. Let it be. Make it so.

Until then, we are borne by the grace of God. He has come to the world in Jesus Christ to give himself freely, for that is the meaning of grace. May it be with all his people, and through them flow into the world.

PRAYER
Amen. Come, Lord Jesus.

Genesis
Henry Wansbrough

Genesis is the story of our beginning. The story of the human race and the whole of creation—and its relationship with the God who is Creator and Lover. As we read and understand those early stories we read and understand our own, and discover more and more about the nature and the love of God the Redeemer.

Dom Henry Wansbrough, OSB, is one of the three General Editors of The People's Bible Commentary.

Mark
R.T. France

In the media and academic circles people still ask questions about a man born 2,000 years ago in Palestine. Who did Jesus think he was? What has his life *then* got to do with our lives *now*? Mark's Gospel answers both those questions, and his 'biography' of Jesus dramatically introduces us to the life and ideas of the person he describes as 'Jesus Christ, the Son of God.'

The Revd Dr R.T. France, formerly Principal of Wycliffe Hall in Oxford, is now Rector of a group of parishes in the Diocese of Hereford.

Galatians
John Fenton

Do we live the Christian life by being very good and keeping a whole set of rules and regulations? That is what the Christians in Galatia asked as well. They had monumentally misunderstood the Christian gospel, and Paul is amazed at their foolishness: 'No!' It's by faith that we start the Christian life, and by faith that we live it—in the Spirit and in union with Christ. A life of astonishing freedom for the Galatians and for us—and Paul's letter to them can guide us in it, too.

The Revd Canon John Fenton is a New Testament scholar, a Canon Emeritus of Christ Church, Oxford, and author of The Matthew Passion *(BRF, 1996).*

1 Corinthians
Jerome Murphy-O'Connor

Here is a description of the divisions and sins of a young church—all of them just the same as those in our Church today. Here are solutions and ways to change and repent, so that the Church, the body of Christ, grows up and builds itself up in love. All that Paul says to them, about 'the Lord's supper', spiritual maturity and spiritual gifts, is relevant to us now.

Jerome Murphy-O'Connor teaches at the École Biblique, Jerusalem.

THE PEOPLE'S BIBLE COMMENTARY VOUCHER SCHEME

The People's Bible Commentary (PBC) provides a range of readable, accessible commentaries. These will grow into a library that will eventually cover the whole Bible.

A voucher is printed on the last page of each People's Bible Commentary Volume (as above). These vouchers count towards free copies of other volumes in the series.

• 4 purchases of PBC volumes entitle the reader to a further volume (up to the value of £7.99) FREE

• 6 purchases of PBC volumes entitle the reader to a further volume (up to the value of £9.99) FREE

Please find the coupon for the PBC voucher scheme overleaf.

All you need do:

• Cut out the appropriate vouchers from the last page of the PBCs you have purchased and attach them to the coupon.

• Complete your name and address details, and indicate your choice of free entitlement from the list on the coupon.

• Take the coupon to your local Christian Bookshop who will exchange it for your free PBC volume; or send the coupon direct to BRF who will send you your free PBC volume. Please allow 28 days for delivery.

Please note that PBC volumes provided under the voucher scheme are subject to availability. If your first choice is not available, you may be sent your second choice volume.

BRF, Peter's Way, Sandy Lane West, Oxford OX4 5HG
Tel 01865 748227 Fax 01865 773150 Registered Charity No. 233280

1.	2.	3.	4.
FREE ENTITLEMENT ONE PBC VOLUME UP TO THE VALUE OF £7.99	5.	6.	FREE ENTITLEMEN ONE PBC VOLUME UP T THE VALUE (£9.99

TO BE COMPLETED BY THE CUSTOMER

My choice of free PBC volume is (please indicate your first and second choice, as all volumes are supplied subject to availability):

Genesis ____
Mark ____
1 Corinthians ____
Galatians ____
Revelation ____
Other (please indicate) ____

Name: ....
Address: ....
....
Postcode: ....

TO BE COMPLETED BY THE BOOKSELL

(Please complete the following. Coupons redee ed will be credited to your account for the valu the book(s) supplied as indicated above. Please note that only coupons correctly completed wit original vouchers will be accepted for credit.):

Name: ....
Address: ....
....
Postcode: ....
Account Number: ....

Completed coupons should be sent to:
BRF, PBC Voucher Scheme, Peter's Way
Sandy Lane West, OXFORD OX4 5HG